Passionate Palate

Recipes for
Romance and Rapture

By Ailene Eberhard
Art by Eric Eberhard

Ailene Eberhard

Manufactured in the United States of America. This edition published by Via Press, 3033 East Turney Avenue, Phoenix, Arizona 85016, 602/957-1955, 800/2 VIA NOW (800/284-2669)

10 9 8 7 6 5 4 3 2

ISBN 1-885001-11-8

Editors: Karla Olson
                      Ora Mae Leffard
Front Cover Painting: Eric Eberhard
Back Cover Design: Lisa Liddy

First edition published 1997 by Soleb of Arizona

For comments, questions, or additional orders contact:

Passionate Palate
P.O. Box 129
Tonto Basin, AZ 85553

Table of Contents

Special thanks to my husband, Eric Eberhard,
for his encouragement and his beautiful art,
which inspires me every day.

This book is lovingly dedicated to our parents
Rosalie and Sheldon Soladar / Evelyn and Milton Eberhard

Also thanks to the families:
Bonni, Frank,
Joshua, Allegra, Kirk, Chad, Todd, Al Grey, Gurumayi,
Anne, Gordon, Pamela, Marilyn, Norman, Stan,
Max, Sharon, Abbe, Scott, Karla, Lisa, Ora Mae,
Willa and Doug,
P.P.O. Linda,
Jeannie,
and Marge.

Introduction

*"**I love you**"—three words we need to hear often. Imagine the waves of good feelings they send through your partner every time he or she hears, "I love you," as if with these words you reassure one another of your mutual feelings.*

***Romance**—seven letters that arouse so many feelings and memories. Getting to know a special someone who enhances your expressions of sentiment and love. Learning everything you can about that person. Looking forward to catching even a moment with your loved one and planning your time alone together. Sharing experiences and building memories. Supping together and discovering what flavors and textures, temperatures and colors excite you both. Talking of future plans and day-to-day events. All of these activities and so many more are the things of which romance is made.*

Yet in our busy, hectic lives, it is hard to remember to take the time to say, "I love you" as often as we should. It seems so simple, yet preoccupied with a million things to do, such as rushing off to a meeting, loading the kids into the car, saying "I love you" slips to the bottom of the priority list. Soon, love may lose some of the excitement and glimmer that it once had. It does not have to be that way. With a tiny bit of effort and a little imagination, you can keep rekindling the romance in your life. Start by recognizing that there are many ways to say, "I love you." A touch on the hand, a parting kiss, a short note tucked into a briefcase or purse, or a lovingly prepared meal can say so much with so little effort.

Mealtime is one part of life that is a natural for romantic infusion. Chances are, your relationship began "over dinner," then progressed through a "getting acquainted" period that extended over numerous meals. Now it is the natural time in the day to regroup, refuel, and share events and observations of the day. Passionate Palate shows that with just a little effort, you can make each meal as romantic as the very first you and your partner shared.

In Passionate Palate, Ailene Eberhard captures the excitement and rewards of exploring passion and romance through food. She understands that preparing a simple, delicious meal for her loved one is one of the most romantic things she can do any day. She sees that mealtime can provide renewal, a time when she and her husband are sure to come together. She has learned that with just a little effort—and some great recipes—any meal, either formal or casual, at a table with candlelight or under a tree with paper napkins, can be a special memory and a romantic moment.

Here are over 25 menus, featuring over 100 delicious, tried-and-true recipes from Ailene's alluring kitchen. They follow the season, since the passage of time with a loved one and the changes that come in a relationship as it grows and develops is very romantic. Using the freshest seasonal foods also makes cooking simpler and even more delicious. Trying new tastes and preparations adds spice and interest, while welcoming back seasonal favorites becomes a celebration in itself. Ailene also encourages tailoring the setting and presentation of the meal to the season and the food itself. Serve hearty winter stew from a sourdough bread bowl in front of the fire. Present fresh trout by the creek in which it was caught.

The pages of Passionate Palate are beautifully enhanced by the moving artwork of renowned artist, Eric Eberhard, Ailene's husband and partner in all things of the heart. Eberhard's stunning cover captures the atmosphere of the seasons and invites the reader to step into the heart and soul of the book. Eberhard has also created a fade-out motif of two wine glasses getting more and more empty as the book progresses.

Passionate Palate begins with some guidelines and hints for infusing romance and love into every meal and every day. Take time to say, "I love you." Never go to bed angry, and look on your partner's actions as optimistically as possible. If you are busy but your partner wants to talk, acknowledge your partner's need and set a time when you can devote your attention to one another. Read together and exchange thoughts about the book you are sharing. These are but a few of Ailene's easy-to-accomplish loving ideas that make all the difference.

On a grander scale, plan ahead for time together, whether it is a well-deserved vacation or a Friday night meal. Keep wish lists on the refrigerator. Make sure your list includes both dream items—a weekend in Paris—and attainable suggestions—a bouquet of tulips in spring.

Ailene has wonderful ideas for simple and delicious preparation and presentation. Basically, stick to healthy preparation of the freshest foods available. This is one of the best ways to say, "I love you and I want you to be with me for a long, long time."

Ailene writes about the long-standing relationship between romance and food, as well as aphrodisiacs and their amazing power to move. From oysters to strawberries, some alluring foods are obvious and enticing while others are mysterious. Ailene encourages you to experiment and discover for yourselves.

In five inspiring chapters, Ailene lays out her formula for year-round romance. Focusing on the seasons and the special occasions that come with each passing year, she presents menus, recipes, and presentation suggestions for over 25 meals. From succulent lamb chops in spring to fresh salmon in summer, from delicate but delectable Cornish game hens in autumn to hearty Bouillabaisse in winter, these meals will entice any reader.

In an important appendix, Ailene offers recipe troubleshooting and save-the-meal suggestions. When you have planned for and anticipate a romantic evening, a soup that is too salty, a lumpy white sauce, or burned rice can really ruin the mood. Here are lifesaving tips from her many years' of experience.

Whether you use this book for special occasions, such as an anniversary when you want the dinner to be perfect, or draw on Ailene's inspiration and make romantic meals part of your every day life, Passionate Palate overflows with inspiring insight and delectable flavors. Enjoy, and remember, the only rules that count in your partnership in cooking is the culinary romance that you share.

By: Karla Olson —Editor

Chapter One
Everyday Romance:

Guidelines For Romantic Living

Cherished Monthly Moments

January   *Start the New Year with candlelight dinners.*

February   *Write special notes and put them on your loved one's pillow at night before your partner comes to bed.*

March   *Surprise your loved one for lunch with a gourmet basket of treats from your kitchen.*

April   *Place fresh flowers around your partner's favorite area to celebrate Spring.*

May   *Feed your loved one peeled grapes while sitting on a comfortable couch.*

June   *Go on a picnic by a lake.*

July   *On the 4th, remember to make a platter of cut star fruit; serve with homemade ice cream.*

August   *Take an afternoon break after serving lunch in bed.*

September   *Go for an afternoon drive to see the magnificent fall colors.*

October   *Spend a weekend at a country inn a few hours from home.*

November   *Experiment to find some new mealtime specials that will excite your partner's palate, use candlelight and fresh flowers on the dinner table when serving.*

December   *Instead of waiting for the holidays, bring them in early and do it your way; celebrate life together each day, say thank you to your partner and to God for every special moment.*

...And remember to always say "I love you" throughout the year!

Romancing Each Other

*In my home, even when we are most disturbed with one another, we say **I love you**. No matter how badly one may feel, hearing those words will make both of you feel better.*

OPTIMISM

Look with optimism towards the behavior of your loved ones. One way to become optimistic quickly is to remember that it can always be worse. Understanding with an open heart and optimistic outlook will make any day better. Each of us is capable of that if we just take the time for one another.

WHEN PARTING FOR A FEW HOURS

*It is often suggested that, **when parting for a few hours for work or sleep**, the sayings, "Don't go to bed upset" or "Don't send your partner off for the day angry," hold true. This applies to most people. Hug your partner and say **I LOVE YOU** before parting for the day. No matter what transpires during the day, your partner will look forward to coming home to you. Whether your partner works in an office or not, we all have stress in our lives. Reach a compromise on the day's problems before falling asleep at night, then bedtime will be a time for fun and rest.*

WISH LISTS

***Wish Lists** are fun! Each of you should keep track of places you wish to visit or attend. Write down gifts you wish to receive. My husband and I post our wish lists on the refrigerator, since we use the refrigerator every day. Fulfilling each other's wishes will create that extra spark of excitement we each look forward to in our lives.*

PLANNING FOR SHARING

If your lives are very hectic, **PLAN** *your calendars to allow adequate time for each other. Consider:*

- *Winter weekends at your favorite romantic hideaway*
- *Sports, such as tennis, golf, skiing, boating*
- *Buy two tickets to a tennis match, basketball or football game*
- *Invite a few couples over for a barbecue in your yard*
- *Go for a Sunday brunch for two at your favorite restaurant*
- *Go to a holiday formal gathering*
- *Buy two tickets to a concert or show*

Many of these usually have to be scheduled in advance. Decide together what you'd like to do during your fun time.

During the summer, our favorite time together is spent going up to our hillside to watch the sunset. During the winter, we often take a glass of hot brandy out on the edge of our cliff and sit in our hot tub to watch the sunset.

You'll find that planning time together—wherever or whatever you choose—will allow you both to prepare for romantic relaxation and fun.

READ BOOKS WITH ONE ANOTHER

Select a book in which you have a shared interest. For instance, adventure books appeal to both of us. We like to read about real life of people during the pioneering days; the adventures people such as the Native Americans had as they met new pioneers; or how the pioneers dealt with the difficult dialect of the new people with which they came in contact.

Take turns reading to each other.

For fun, try visualizing yourselves as the characters in the book; it gives more life to a story. Of course, if you're choosing a murder mystery novel, the theatrics should be left out, **please***!*

TAKE TIME OUT TO LISTEN TO EACH OTHER AT MEALTIME

For many of us, mealtime is the only time of the day when we can sit and talk with each other. Take advantage of that time and give your loved one the time needed to express feelings. Being able to LISTEN to each other is a great gift. If your loved one is speaking to you and you're caught up in your own thoughts, make a note to remind yourself of your thoughts. That way, you'll be a full listener to your partner.

ANYTIME

We're all very busy in our daily lives. So much to do—so little time. Even when we're not busy with projects outside the home, we all manage to find enough little things to keep us busy. Some of the most important recipes to a healthy marriage:

- *Take a break from what you're doing when a loved one needs a listening partner.*
- *Take a break to be with a loved one, not just for that serious moment, but also to have fun together. A "kiss break" is always nice!*

At an unnerving time, such as when you're in the middle of an important project and your partner needs to speak with you, take a minute and agree to a future moment together as soon as you can.

Remember to be there for your partner.

IGNORE WHAT YOU CAN

When your partner has a lot on the calendar for that day and forgets to help you with something you needed, remember the times when your partner was there for you.

Remember, we all have those moments. Ignore the rudeness and tell your partner to have a good day. Say, "I love you," and let your partner know that you need help with something later that day.

When your partner calls you during the day and sounds irritated, don't take it personally. Dealing with a day may be frustrating. Your partner is most likely calling you to have you listen. Concentrate on listening and comforting your partner. Most likely, any anger is not directed at you.

When a partner is late without calling you for the first time, ignore the anger you may feel for a moment while you ask what kept him or her. Ask for a phone call next time.

If a partner is late often without notice to you, offer to meet him or her at the end of the work day at the office. Maybe some organizational support from you is needed.

If your partner seems to be ignoring your needs, quietly remind him or her of those needs.

Keep as calm as you can at all times. Nobody ever profits in any way from a temper driven conversation. One way or another, everything works out in time. **IGNORE** *the things that annoy you if they aren't important enough to cause any harm.*

Be happy for what you are! Be happy for what you have! *The way we see things is quite clear. All of us have choices to make every day of our lives. Whatever our situation, we each have to decide whether to take the easy road **or** to put a little effort into our lives. By choosing to do your best, you'll always be thankful each day for what you **do have!** It's easy to sit back and look at all the sad things that exist. Instead, take a moment and give thanks...*

- *For seeing the sky*

- *Hearing a bird chirp*

- *Having enough water to water our crops*

- *Or being happy just for a new day,*

Live with a cup half full, *not half empty.*

TODAY

Live for today. Do one thing for yourself that is satisfying enough to you, and do one thing for some other person. Simple things, like:

- *Opening a door for somebody else*
- *Lifting a child to get a drink of water from a fountain*
- *Allowing somebody in a rush to cut ahead of you in line without getting upset.*

Life is short. Our time with a loved one is limited. So take advantage of being blessed with each other each day. All we have is today. Tomorrow is in God's hands and yesterday is gone.

Anniversary Ideas For Romance & Rapture

- *Go camping in the mountains. Bring wine, roses, and candlelight. Make a picnic dinner and relax under the stars.*

- *Make a special dinner together. Try the Sushi dinner on page 98.*

- *Go fishing for the day and barbecue your catch for dinner. Try the recipe on page 52. Serve wine and enjoy being together.*

- *Visit a beach town for the weekend. After a fabulous dinner at your favorite beachside restaurant, take a moonlight walk on the beach.*

- *After you've been married awhile, renew your vows. Have a party with 50 of your closest friends to celebrate.*

- *Take a flight for the weekend to your honeymoon site. It may be under new ownership, but you can still recreate that first romantic night together.*

- *Go hiking in your favorite mountain location. (We love Jackson Hole, Wyoming. We were married in the mountains there and we hiked to Lake of the Crags* the day before!)*

- *Surprise your partner and hire a driver to take you both to one of your partner's fantasy places.*

- *Dress up in your fanciest clothes, open a bottle of champagne, and celebrate your wedding vows by watching your wedding tape or looking at wedding pictures together.*

*Lake of the Crags is the highest Alpine lake in the Tetons of Wyoming.

Aphrodisiacs to Enhance Your Love Life

Apricot is a love food.

Caviar gives aphrodisiac powers.

Chocolate will excite you.

Deer meat adds strength and virility.

Eggs are good for procreation; however, too many may lead to promiscuity.

Figs give luscious feelings.

Garlic aids in circulation of all body parts.

Ginseng for longevity.

Guava for passion.

Honey for endearment.

Muscles and oysters—feed them to each other for prolonged foreplay.

Onion improves sexual endurance.

Peach is the "love food".

Pomegranates have red seeds of fertility.

Radishes enhance ecstasy.

Rice for fertility.

Royal jelly brings high self esteem.

Seaweed brings more lust to your lovemaking.

Strawberries great for sharing.

Tomato or "love apple".

Whipped cream—used for a "dip" to entice one another.

The Times That Memories Are Made From

OUR LOVE WAS BORN

_____

_____

_____

_____

_____

_____

OUR FIRST MOST MEMORABLE DAY

_____ *At* _____

We _____

_____

_____

_____

_____

_____

MEMORABLE DATES

_____

_____

_____

_____

_____

OUR FAVORITE RESTAURANTS

MONDAY _____

TUESDAY _____

WEDNESDAY _____

THURSDAY _____

FRIDAY _____

SATURDAY _____

SUNDAY _____

ANY DAY _____

_____

OUR SPECIAL PLACES FOR OUTINGS TOGETHER

_____

_____

_____

_____

_____

_____

OUR FAVORITE SPORTS TO DO TOGETHER

_____

_____

_____

_____

_____

ROMANTIC VACATIONS

_____

_____

_____

_____

_____

_____

_____

_____

_____

_____

_____

FUTURE HOPES AND DREAMS

_____

_____

_____

_____

_____

_____

_____

_____

_____

_____

A WISH LIST FOR EACH OF YOU!

*NAME*_____   *NAME*_____

*An Elegant Dinner for 2*_____   *An Elegant Dinner for 2*_____

_____   _____

_____   _____

_____   _____

_____   _____

_____   _____

_____   _____

_____   _____

_____   _____

_____   _____

_____   _____

_____   _____

_____   _____

_____   _____

_____   _____

_____   _____

_____   _____

_____   _____

_____   _____

ANNIVERSARIES

Gifts   Experiences

1st_____   _____

2nd_____   _____

3rd_____   _____

4th_____   _____

5th_____   _____

6th_____   _____

7th_____   _____

8th_____   _____

9th_____   _____

10th_____   _____

15th_____   _____

20th_____   _____

25th_____   _____

30th_____   _____

40th_____   _____

50th_____   _____

60th_____   _____

70th_____   _____

75th_____   _____

Partnership

Not just caring
Not just being together
Not just saying "I love you"

Believing in the same goals
Believing in each other's goals
Believing in what each of us dream for
Helping to decide what to go for

Not telling each other what is right
Not saying yes or no

Believing in all these values as a whole
That is what we give our souls to

A union with each other
A union in one with God and Nature
A union in one with the universe

That is what we both give to each other

Serving each other
For each other
For us together each and as a whole.

God Bless!

Chapter Two: Hearts Filled with Spring

Lentil Soup
Rosemary and Garlic Lamb Chops in the Garden
Tomato and Onion
Brussels Sprouts and Cauliflower
Rosemary Bread
Pecan Pie

Vegetable/Cabbage Soup
Coho Salmon
Fried Green Tomatoes
Simple Baked Potato or Yam
Olive Loaf
Crepes

Smoked Oysters on Crackers
Shrimp Mousse
Mesculin Salad
Frozen Grapes

Asparagus Chicken with Oriental Barbecue Sauce Dip
Glazed Carrots
Basmati Rice
Herb Breads
Vanilla Ice Cream with Berries, Kumquats, or Granola Topping

Leg of Lamb
Baby-sized Vegetables
Garlic and Parmesan Potatoes
Sourdough Rolls
Fruitified Cheesecake

Sweet 'n' Sour Tofu
Zucchini Kiss
Dill Herbed Rice
Lemon Pie

Vegetarian Lasagna
Basil Bread
Vanilla Cake with Swiss Mocha Topping

Lentil Soup

~

Rosemary and Garlic Lamb Chops
in the Garden

~

Tomato and Onion

~

Brussels Sprouts and Cauliflower

~

Rosemary Bread

~

Pecan Pie

Lentil Soup

1 tablespoon olive oil
2 large garlic cloves, minced
3/4 cup chopped chives
1/2 teaspoon salt
2 teaspoons pepper
4 medium carrots, diced
2 cups beef broth (see recipe below)
1 cup lentils
4 cups water
1/4 cup chopped parsley

Heat oil in a large pot over medium heat. Add garlic, chives, salt, pepper, and carrots and sauté about 5 minutes. Add the beef stock, lentils, and water. Bring to a boil, then cover and reduce heat. Simmer for 1 hour or until the lentils are tender.

For a thicker soup, place two cups of the cooked soup in the blender. Blend on low for 1 minute, then return blended mixture to the original soup.

Sprinkle each serving with chopped parsley.

For chicken or beef broth: (Whenever I cook a roast beef or make roast chicken, I prepare a broth first, then freeze it for use in recipes later. Partially cooking meats makes the roasting process go quicker, too.)

Beef roast or roasting chicken
Water to cover
1/4 teaspoon salt
1/2 teaspoon pepper
1 clove garlic, minced

Place meat in a large soup pot and cover with water. cover and bring to a boil, then simmer for 1 hour. Remove beef or chicken from pot and set aside for roasting. Skim fat off top of stock, then simmer, uncovered, for 30 minutes more to reduce stock. Remove stock from heat and let cool. Pour into ice cube trays and freeze overnight. Remove from trays and place in an airtight container. Stock will keep in the freezer for up to six months.

Rosemary and Garlic Lamb Chops in the Garden

2 large garlic cloves, minced
1 teaspoon salt
1 teaspoon pepper
1 tablespoon olive oil
4 sprigs fresh rosemary
4 double loin lamb chops

Preheat oven to 375 °. In a small bowl, combine garlic, salt, and pepper. Rub the mixture all over the lamb and let stand for 20 minutes. Put oil in pan, making sure entire surface is covered. Lay rosemary sprigs in bottom of pan and lay lamb chops on top of sprigs. Bake chops for 1/2 hour, then turn and cook 1/2 hour longer, or until meat is slightly pink. Serve on a decorative platter with a few sprigs of rosemary as a garnish.

Tomato and Onion

1 extra large tomato, cut into 1/8-inch slices
1 extra large Bermuda onion, cut into 1/8-inch chives
1/2 cup barbecue sauce (see recipe below)
1/8 cup balsamic vinegar
3 tablespoons olive oil
Sprinkle of salt

Alternate and slightly overlap tomato and onion slices around the perimeter of a large plate, leaving one piece of each for the center. Place all other ingredients in a container with a tight-fitting lid and shake well. Pour dressing into a gravy bowl and offer with salad.

For the Barbecue Sauce:
1/2 cup water
3 tablespoons corn syrup
1 6-oz can tomato paste
3/4 cup molasses
1 tablespoon vinegar
Pinch salt
1 teaspoon chives
2 garlic cloves, crushed
Pinch of each: mustard seeds, paprika, turmeric, fresh ground pepper

Combine all ingredients in a saucepan and simmer for 35 minutes.

Brussels Sprouts and Cauliflower

1 medium head of cauliflower
1/2 pound brussels sprouts
2 teaspoons low-sodium soy sauce
4 tablespoons butter
Sprinkle of paprika (for color)

Break cauliflower into florets and cook with brussels sprouts in boiling, salted water for 10 minutes. Drain and toss with soy sauce, butter, and paprika.

Rosemary Bread

This is a simple technique that can be used with any combination of breads and herbs or seasonings. We love to use a sourdough loaf; baguettes, French loaves, whole wheat loaves are also delicious. We used any of the following herbs and seasonings in all kinds of combinations: dill, oregano, rosemary, garlic, parmesan cheese, basil, black pepper. Experiment and see what pleases your palate.

1 loaf of fresh bread (sourdough, French, whole wheat, or a baguette)
1/4 cup butter
Salt to taste
2 tablespoons dried rosemary

Slice the bread in half lengthwise and spread it open. Spread butter evenly on both halves, then sprinkle with a little salt. For the fullest flavor, crush the rosemary in your palm as you sprinkle it onto the bread.

Pecan Pie

1 cup white corn syrup
3/4 cup dark brown sugar
1/3 cup melted butter
1 heaping cup shelled pecans
3 eggs
1/2 teaspoon vanilla
1/4 teaspoon salt
9-inch unbaked pastry shell

Preheat oven to 350 °. In a large bowl, mix all the ingredients except the pastry shell. Pour mixture into the shell, then bake for 45 to 50 minutes or until slightly brown. Top with whipped cream or ice cream.

Vegetable/Cabbage Soup

~

Coho Salmon

~

Fried Green Tomatoes

~

Simple Baked Potato or Yam

~

Olive Loaf

~

Crepes

Vegetable/Cabbage Soup

1 head cabbage
8 carrots
4 stalks celery
1 stalk broccoli
4 large tomatoes
1/4 cup tomato paste
3 bay leaves
1-1/2 teaspoon chili powder
1 teaspoon canola margarine
1/2 teaspoon curry powder

Cut all above vegetables into chunks. Put into pot and cover with water. Bring the water to a boil, cover and simmer 1 hour and 25 minutes.

Coho Salmon

2 Coho salmon (one fish per person)
Fresh rosemary twigs (large bunch)
1/2 cup canola oil
1/2 cup water
Pinch of salt and pepper

Preheat oven to 375. Rub whole fish with oil, salt, and pepper. Lay half of the twigs in pan with 1/2 cup of water. Take each whole fish and fill cavity with a bunch of twigs and sew middle seam of fish together. Lay whole stuffed fish on top of twigs in pan. Cover with foil and cook for 25 minutes per pound.

Fried Green Tomatoes

1 large firm solid green tomato sliced into 1/8-inch slices for every 2 people
1/4 cup flour
1/2 teaspoon salt
1 teaspoon pepper
1/4 cup canola oil

Heat oil over medium heat. Mix together flour, salt, and pepper in a plastic bag. Put tomato slices gently into bag and shake until tomato slices are well covered. Lay tomatoes into hot oiled pan and fry until brown. Turn after 3 minutes to brown other side.

This dish is a gourmet delight with any fish or southern style meal. We eat them whenever we can find them in our market place. It's a rare finding up here in the mountain states!

Simple Baked Potato or Baked Yam

Wash potatoes of your choice. Preheat oven to 450°. Pierce each potato with a fork 3 times and place potatoes on cookie sheet in oven. Cook for 45 minutes. Serve with canola margarine or sour cream and chives.

Olive Loaf (see page 86)

Crepes

4 eggs
3/4 cups milk
3/4 cups flour
1/2 teaspoon salt
1 tablespoon canola oil

Combine milk, eggs, flour, and salt. Mix with wire whisk until smooth. Over medium heat, heat one tablespoon oil. Pour about 3 tablespoons of batter into hot pan and tilt pan to coat bottom. Cook until top is set and bottom is lightly browned. Flip crepe to brown on other side. Serve with ice cream and hot fudge sauce, or any way you like it. Try fresh fruit for a refreshing treat!

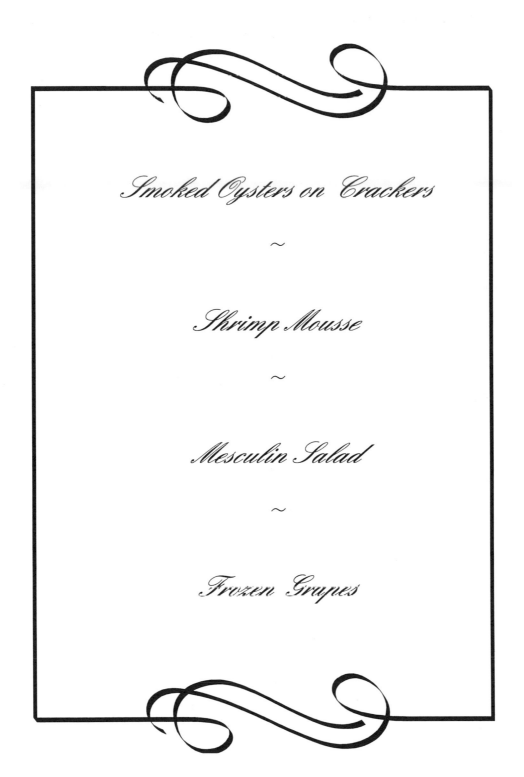

Smoked Oysters on Crackers

~

Shrimp Mousse

~

Mesculin Salad

~

Frozen Grapes

Smoked Oysters on Crackers

Your favorite cracker will do.

Canned smoked oysters (try buying low salt packed in canola oil).

Open can of oysters and drain, then blot out oil on paper towels. Lay crackers out on a plate and place one oyster per cracker and serve.

Shrimp Mousse

1 can tomato soup
2 8-oz. package cream cheese
2 envelopes gelatin
1/3 cup cold water
1 cup canola mayonnaise
3/4 cup finely chopped celery
3/4 cup finely chopped chives
2 cups cleaned and deveined medium shrimp, mashed
1 tablespoon Worcestershire sauce
3 tablespoons lemon juice

Soak gelatin in water. Heat soup to boiling and add cream cheese and gelatin. Cool. Add all other ingredients and mix. Pour into mold and chill for several hours before serving.

Mesculine Salad

1 cup of mesculine leaves per person.

This is a very expensive salad. Use small portions, well cleaned, from your local fresh vegetable source. Serve with any dressing of your choice. We like the plain leaves on a salad plate sprinkled with a little fresh lemon juice or balsamic vinegar. Try adding a little bit of fresh ground pepper.

Frozen Grapes

Buy grapes without seeds. Any color grape will be delicious frozen. After returning from supermarket, wash grapes and set aside on paper towel to dry. Once thoroughly dry, place whole, including stem, in plastic freezing sack. Take grapes out to eat as desired. Never defrost them first because they will be soggy. Frozen they taste like little popsicles and the fun you'll have tantalizing each other while you slowly feed each other one frozen grape at a time.

*Asparagus Chicken with
Oriental Barbecue Sauce Dip*

~

Glazed Carrots

~

Basmati Rice

~

Herb Breads

~

*Vanilla Ice Cream with Berries,
Kumquats, or Granola Topping*

Asparagus Chicken with Oriental Barbecue Sauce Dip

2 chicken breasts
1 bunch asparagus
10 mushrooms
1/2 cup canola oil
1/2 cup oriental barbecue sauce

Roll the asparagus and mushrooms into the chicken breasts. Use toothpicks to hold in place. Heat canola oil and add oriental barbecue sauce. Sauté the rolled chicken. For a stronger flavor, first marinate the rolled chicken in teriyaki sauce overnight, then cook.

Oriental Barbecue Sauce

1/2 cup water
1 tablespoon of corn syrup
6 oz. tomato paste
6 oz molasses
1 tablespoon chives
Pinch of salt
1 teaspoon chives
Pinch of mustard seed
Pinch of paprika
3 garlic cloves, crushed
Pinch of tumeric
Pinch of pepper

Cook above ingredients and simmer 35 minutes. Use on any of your favorite oriental dishes.

Glazed Carrots

3 large carrots, peeled
2 tablespoons canola margarine

Slice carrots; steam for 20 minutes. Remove carrots from steamer pan and add canola margarine back into pan, then fold in carrots. Cook for 2 minutes. The margarine will give the carrots a slight glaze.

Basmati Rice

1 cup of basmati rice
1-3/4 cups hot water
1 teaspoon canola margarine
Pinch of salt

Sauté rice in margarine until brown. Add hot water and salt. Cover and steam rice for 20 minutes, or until water is absorbed.

Herb Breads

Herb breads are easy and taste delicious. You may either buy or make a fresh loaf of sourdough (our favorite), baguette, French, or whole wheat loaves.

Slice the bread in half to open it up. Spread canola margarine evenly on both open halves. Sprinkle a little salt, then either/or

Garlic and Parmesan cheese and then oregano sprinkled slightly on top

Dill	Oregano	Rosemary	Garlic	Basil	Black Pepper

You can have a lot of fun experimenting. Remember that when using herbs, you'll get the full flavor of the herb by placing it in your hand and sifting the herb between your hands. You do this by rubbing your hands together as you sprinkle the herbs onto the loaves.

Vanilla Ice Cream with Berries, Kumquats or Granola Topping

Store-bought is easiest (unless of course you own one of those fabulous ice-cream makers). I try to use low-fat ice cream. Otherwise, for that once-in-awhile time when you feel like staying home and slaving to your freezer, try this home-made recipe that works:

4 cups of milk
1/3 cup flour
3/4 cup sugar
1/4 teaspoon salt
4 cups whipped cream (if you're going this far already, make home-made)
5 beaten eggs
2 teaspoons vanilla

Cook milk, flour, sugar, and salt until thick. Chill until completely cooled. Once cooled, add whipped cream, eggs, and vanilla. Beat well with electric mixer. Place in shallow pan in freezer until mix becomes firm. Remove from freezer after mix becomes firm and beat again. Repeat freezing and beating four more times; then store in covered freezer bowl. You can also add 1 cup of crushed fruit, such as strawberries, when you add the vanilla for a variation.

Leg of Lamb

~

Baby-sized Vegetables

~

Garlic and Parmesan Potatoes

~

Sourdough Rolls

~

Fruitified Cheesecake

Leg of Lamb

Back 1/2 leg (wider Half) of lamb, or full leg of lamb if serving more than six persons
1-1/2 to 2 cups plain yogurt
1/2 cup Dijon mustard
1 tablespoon garlic
Salt to taste

Preheat oven to 375°. Wash and pat dry leg of lamb. Rub garlic, salt, and pepper into lamb. Then rub mustard into lamb. Coat entire leg with yogurt. This seals in the juices. Place lamb on pan in oven and cook 20 minutes per pound. Serve to the pure delight of your partner and/or guests!

Baby-sized Vegetables

1 cup miniature carrots
1 cup miniature zucchini
1 cup of whatever you can find and are interested in using in your miniature vegetable side dish
Dash of pepper

Steam your vegetables and serve whole on pretty side dishes with a dash of pepper. If in season, they are very sweet and delicious!

Garlic and Parmesan Potatoes

6 Idaho potatoes, sliced thin
2 garlic cloves, minced
2 tablespoons canola margarine
Fresh minced chives
2 tablespoons grated Parmesan cheese

Preheat oven to 350°. Put the potatoes in a baking pan and arrange so the potatoes barely touch each other. Sprinkle with garlic. Dot with margarine and sprinkling of chives. Sprinkle with Parmesan cheese and cook for 35 minutes or until mildly brown.

Sourdough Rolls

From your local bakery

Frutified Cheesecake

2 8-oz. packages cream cheese
1/2 cup sugar or sugar substitute
1 cup fresh raspberries, blueberries, or strawberries
1/2 teaspoon vanilla
2 eggs
2 cups graham cracker crumbs
1/3 cup melted canola margarine
1 8-oz. round baking tin

Preheat oven to 350°. Melt margarine in tin and crush graham cracker crumbs into margarine to form a moist crust. In a separate bowl, mix cream cheese, sugar, and vanilla until well blended. Add eggs and blend 3 more minutes on medium speed. Carefully stir 1/2 of the fruit into the mix. Pour cream cheese mix into pie shell, top with remaining fruit and bake at 350° for 40 minutes.

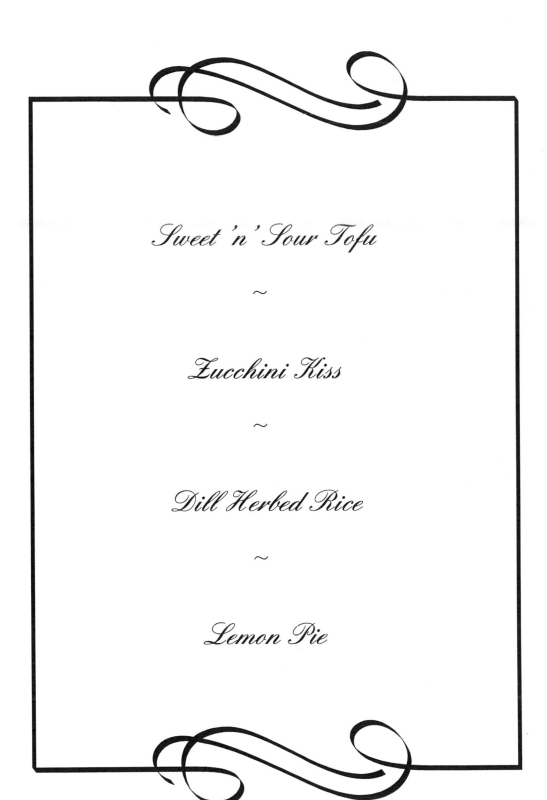

Sweet 'n' Sour Tofu

~

Zucchini Kiss

~

Dill Herbed Rice

~

Lemon Pie

Sweet 'n' Sour Tofu

1 pound Tofu, drained and cubed
1/2 cup chives, diced
2 carrots, diced
2 zucchini, diced
3 stalks of celery
3 peppers cut into small chunks

Sauce
1/3 cup honey
1 tablespoon cider vinegar
2 tablespoons cornstarch
1/2 cup cold water
2 tablespoon ginger

Mix ingredients together except cornstarch with a whisk. When smooth, add cornstarch and whisk again for 2 minutes or until smooth.

or **Sweet 'n' Sour Sauce**
1/2 cup chives
1/2 cup barbecue sauce
15-1/2 oz. jar of peach preserves
1 tablespoon tempera sauce
1 can water chestnuts, sliced

Heat barbecue sauce, peach preserves, tempura sauce together. Add other ingredients and cook ten minutes.

In wok or large pan, fry tofu. Add vegetables in this order, cooking a little at a time: chives, celery, carrots, zucchini, pepper. Sauté until crisp. Make a hole in the middle. Mix sauce again and pour into center. Mix well over high heat until thick, then remove from heat and stir with food.

Zucchini Kiss

This delicious dish may be used as a side or main event.

1 pkg pull-apart biscuits, peeled apart and rolled to 1/4 inch thickness
10 whole raw almonds
5 medium zucchini, sliced and steamed until soft
pinch each garlic, tarragon, salt (optional), pepper
1/2 teaspoon mustard
3 egg whites
3/4 cup shredded mozzarella or Monterey Jack cheese

Preheat oven to 325°. Line the bottom and sides of a 9-inch pie plate with the biscuits. Press almonds into the biscuits. Mix zucchini with garlic, tarragon, salt, and pepper and set aside. Mix mustard with egg whites and pour over zucchini. Pour egg/zucchini mixture into pie plate and top with shredded cheese. Bake for 45 minutes or until top is browned.

Dill Herbed Rice

Herbed rice is made by using the recipe on page 34 for Basmati rice, then adding fresh dill into the hot water for flavoring. Other ideas are to add:

Vegetable bullion cubes	Beef bullion cubes
Fresh cilantro	Fresh rosemary
Fresh dill	

Lemon Pie

2 large beaten eggs
2 egg whites
1/2 cup sugar
1 large lemon, peel and all
3 tablespoons butter or substitute
1 9-inch unbaked pie shell

Liquefy all ingredients (except pie shell) in blender. Pour into pie shell and bake in a conventional oven at 350° for about 40 minutes, or bake in a convection oven at 300-325° for about 40 minutes.

Simple Pie Crust (or buy one at the supermarket) There are so many to choose from these days. The graham cracker ones are our favorite and less messy than doing it fresh at home. Of course, home-made crusts don't have chemical preservatives which really aren't very good for us!)

2 cups flour
2/3 cup shortening
1 teaspoon salt
1 egg yolk
1/2 teaspoon vinegar

Combine flour and salt in a large bowl. Add shortening and work until flour mixture is crumbly. Put the egg yolk in a measuring cup and fill with enough water to make 1/2 cup. Add vinegar. Add to flour mixture and mix until well combined. Roll dough out on a lightly floured surface and roll on one side only. (don't over mix or the pastry will be tough.)

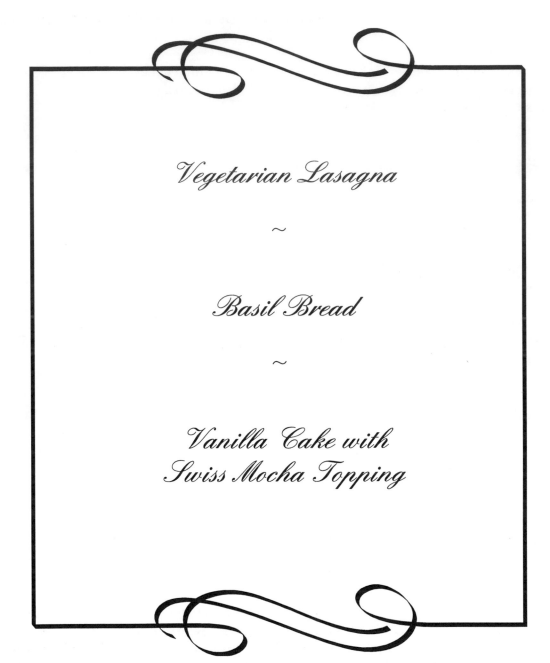

Vegetarian Lasagna

~

Basil Bread

~

Vanilla Cake with
Swiss Mocha Topping

Vegetarian Lasagna *(Terrific!)*

1 box of Lasagna noodles cooked and drained and laid out individually on waxed paper to avoid
    sticking
Tomato Sauce #2
1/2 cup mushroom caps cooked and sliced thin
1 yellow squash cooked and sliced thin
1 zucchini squash cooked and sliced thin
1 yam cooked and sliced thin
1 cup cooked spinach (optional)
16 oz. ricotta cheese
1 cup mozzarella cheese
1/4 cup Parmesan cheese
Sprinkle of oregano

Tomato Sauce #2

3/4 cup of chives, minced
Garlic cloves, minced
Large or 3 small bay leaves
12-oz. can Italian style peeled tomatoes
15-oz can tomato sauce with herbs
6-oz. can tomato paste
1/3 cup canola oil
1/2 cup cream sherry or red cooking wine
1/2 teaspoon sugar
1/3 cup fresh parsley, minced

Sauté chives, garlic, and spices in oil and simmer. Add 2-3 tomatoes. Finely shred the rest
of the tomatoes and add to sauce. Slowly add the rest of the ingredients and simmer for as
many hours as you have available that day. This recipe is big enough to cool and freeze
portions for the next time you're having Italian food. Italian sauces can also be refrigerated
for a few days. It seems they actually taste better the second day.

Preheat oven to 425°. Lay thin layer of sauce in lasagna pan. Lay 5 lasagna noodles out to cover
sauce. Sprinkle Parmesan cheese over noodles, cover with thin layer of sauce, then lay one of
your vegetables out on half the pan, such as zucchini on one side, yellow squash on the other.
cover with cheese. Build layers until all ingredients are used. Cool and cut into 4-inch square
serving pieces.

Basil Bread (see page 35)

Vanilla Cake with Swiss Mocha Topping

Vanilla Cake

2-1/4 cups all purpose flour
3 teaspoons baking powder
1 teaspoon baking soda
1 teaspoon salt
3/4 cup sugar
1/3 cup canola oil
1 cup milk
1 teaspoon vanilla
2 egg yolks
2 egg whites

Preheat oven to 350°. In a large bowl, sift flour, baking powder, baking soda, salt, and 1/2 cup sugar. Make a hole and add oil, milk, and vanilla. Mix. Add egg yolks and mix at medium speed until smooth. In a separate bowl, beat egg whites at high speed. Gradually add 1/4 cup sugar and beat to form stiff peaks. Fold into first mixture and pour into an 8 x 12 inch baking pan. Bake for 30 minutes or until an inserted wooden toothpick comes out clean.

Swiss Mocha Topping

3 tablespoons canola margarine
1 egg yolk
2 tablespoons instant coffee powder
1 tablespoon boiled water
1 cup powdered sugar
2 tablespoons semi-sweet liquid chocolate

Cream margarine and egg yolk until smooth. Stir in chocolate. Dissolve coffee powder in boiling water. Add powdered sugar to margarine mixture and beat well. Slowly add dissolved coffee. Beat until smooth and fluffy.

Chapter Three: Lazy Summer Days of Love

Coho Salmon Creekside
Lavender Rice
Broccoli Casserole
Rosemary Bread
Frozen Papaya

Cream of Broccoli Soup
Chilled Simply Elegant Chicken
Deviled Asparagus
Dill Bread
Berries and Whipped Cream

Cutthroat or Lake Trout
Rainbow Cole Slaw
French Style Green Beans
Corn Chowder
Your Favorite Lemon Sorbet

Barbecued Chicken
Green Salad of Your Choice with Papaya Salad Dressing
Double-Cooked Mashed Potatoes
Quick Dinner Rolls
Pecan Pie

German Fried Chicken
Rainbow Cole Slaw
Fresh Corn off the Cob
Broccoli au Gratin
Apple Crunch Pie

Orange Chicken
Beet Greens
Basmati Rice
Frozen Mango

Beef Kabobs
Cheese Platter
Stuffed Artichoke Hearts
Raspberry Pie a la Mode

Zucchini Penne Italian Bake
Vegetable Platter
Pepper Bread
Orange Pie

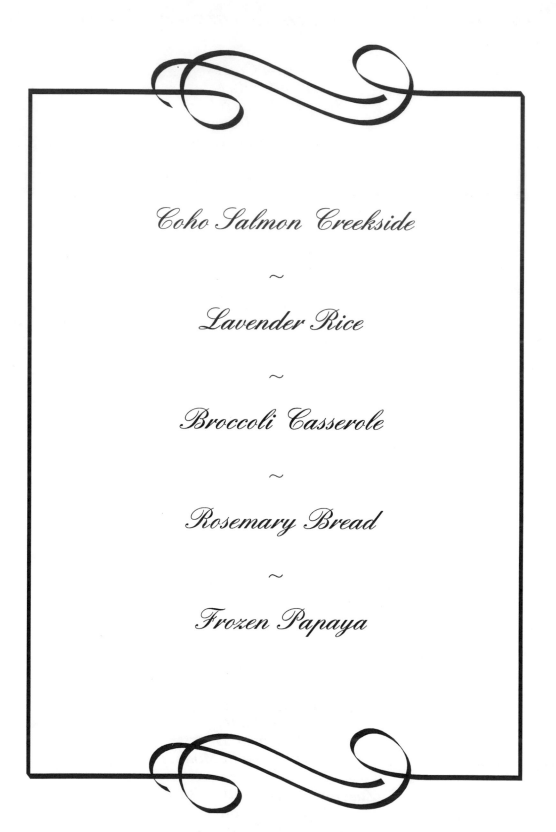

Coho Salmon Creekside

~

Lavender Rice

~

Broccoli Casserole

~

Rosemary Bread

~

Frozen Papaya

Coho Salmon Creekside

2 Coho salmon – individually sized
1/4 cup olive oil
Salt and pepper
Large bunch of fresh rosemary twigs
1/2 cup water

Preheat oven to 375°. Rub whole fish with oil and sprinkle with salt and pepper; then fill cavity with 1/4 of the twigs for each fish. Sew middle cavity closed with a large needle and a double thickness of thread. Lay remaining half of the twigs in a pan large enough to hold the fish, then pour water into bottom of pan. Lay fish on top of the twigs. Cover with foil and bake for 25 minutes per pound. Remove thread before serving.

Lavender Rice

Get fresh lavender buds—just a few—or other available edible flower. Cook Basmati rice - see page 34. When cooked, sprinkle buds for a beautiful presentation and culinary after affect.

Broccoli Casserole

1 head of broccoli
1/2 cup grated Monterey Jack cheese
1/2 can cream of mushroom soup
1/2 cup mayonnaise
1 tablespoon dried chives
1 egg, beaten
1/3 cup grated Parmesan cheese
1/4 cup bread crumbs

Preheat oven to 350°. Break broccoli into florets, then cook in lightly salted water until tender, about 20 minutes. Drain and set aside. Mix other ingredients, except Parmesan cheese and bread crumbs, then mix with broccoli, stirring to coat. Pour mixture into a casserole dish. Mix together Parmesan and bread crumbs, and sprinkle over casserole. Bake for 35 minutes.

Rosemary Bread

Follow the recipe for Dill bread on page 35, using 2 tablespoons of rosemary.

Frozen Papaya

1 papaya, peeled, pitted, and cut into bite-sized cubes

Place cubed papaya in a plastic freezer bag and freeze for at least 3 hours. Serve with toothpicks or use your fingers.

Cream of Broccoli Soup

~

Chilled Simply Elegant Chicken

~

Deviled Asparagus

~

Dill Bread

~

Berries and Whipped Cream

Cream of Broccoli Soup

1 bunch of broccoli, chopped
3 tablespoons chives, chopped
1 cup boiling water with 2 chicken bouillon cubes dissolved
1 tablespoon canola margarine
1/2 tablespoon flour
Pinch of mace
Salt and pepper to taste
1 cup light half and half cream

In a heavy saucepan, combine chives, broccoli, and chicken broth. Bring to a quick boil, then simmer for 15 minutes on low heat until broccoli is tender. Put mixture aside. Melt margarine in saucepan. Add flour and stir until all lumps disappear. Add salt, pepper, and mace, stirring constantly. Now slowly add half and half and stir. Add broccoli mixture and continue cooking over medium heat to a full boil. Simmer 2 minutes and serve.

Chilled Simply Elegant Chicken

3 pound chicken
3 tablespoons rosemary
3 tablespoons tarragon
Pinch of cayenne pepper
1 tablespoon garlic powder

Preheat oven to 300°. Mix spices and coat chicken. Place chicken in covered foil pouch and cook 3 hours. You may also use and store ready/oven ready plastic cooking pouch. Follow the directions on the package for cooking times. When cooked, cover in refrigerator for three hours, then serve. May be served warm.

Deviled Asparagus with Ritz

1 bunch asparagus
1 can cream of mushroom soup
1 small box Ritz cheese crackers
1/2 stick melted canola margarine
1 tablespoon finely diced bell pepper
1 tablespoon finely chopped chives
1 tablespoon pimento
1 teaspoon Worcestershire sauce
1 package toasted almonds

Mix seasonings with the soup. Mix the cracker crumbs with butter. Arrange a buttered casserole dish, using a layer of soup mixture, then asparagus, then crackers. Garnish with almonds. Heat for 30 minutes at 300°.

Dill Bread (see page 35)

Berries of Your Choice

Homemade Whipped Cream

Buy 1 pint of Whipping Cream
Beat at high speed until it thickens and peaks. A teaspoon of sugar may be added, but I never used it. The cream alone is quite tasty!

Cutthroat or Lake Trout

~

Rainbow Cole Slaw

~

French Style Green Beans

~

Corn Chowder

~

Your Favorite Lemon Sorbet

Cutthroat or Lake Trout

1 whole fish per person
1/4 cup canola oil
1/2 cup lite teriyaki or soy sauce
Garlic, pepper, salt to taste

Clean fish thoroughly. Mix all ingredients together and rub into fish; let stand 20 minutes. Wrap fish individually in foil and place on medium hot grill or on pan under broiler for 11 minutes on each side. Hold the fish by the tail and pull the main bones out clean from the fish. The meat falls away from the skin and is delectable!

Rainbow Cole Slaw

1 large head of cabbage (for a change in flavor, try purple or mixed cabbage)
1/2 cup low fat sour cream
1/2 cup vinegar
1 cup low fat mayonnaise
1/2 teaspoon sugar or sugar substitute
1 teaspoon dried dill
1 diced apple
Salt and pepper to taste

Shred cabbage into bowl. Mix other ingredients. Stir cabbage into mix. Cover and marinate for 2 to 3 hours in refrigerator before serving.

French Style Green Beans

1 cup French style green beans
1/4 cup almond slivers
2 tablespoons canola margarine
Dash of salt, pepper, garlic

Sauté almond slivers in margarine for 8 minutes. Add other ingredients and cook 8 minutes more. Serve immediately!

Corn Chowder

1-1/2 oz. pork cubes
1 cup cream style corn
1/2 cup chives, chopped
1/3 cup water
1 cup milk
1/2 rib of celery, chopped
2 tablespoons canola margarine
3/4 cup diced potatoes
1 cup chicken broth
2 tablespoons green pepper, diced
2 tablespoons red pepper, diced
Pepper to taste (optional)

Fry the pork until brown. Add the celery, chives, potatoes, chicken broth, and water; simmer until the potatoes are done. Add the corn and simmer 5 minutes, stirring occasionally. Heat the milk and margarine and add to the soup. Add red and green peppers and turn off heat while you add some pepper to taste. Serve immediately.

Your favorite lemon sorbet is the nicest finish to this delectable meal!

Barbecued Chicken

~

*Green Salad of Your Choice
with Papaya Salad Dressing*

~

Double - Cooked Mashed Potatoes

~

Quick Dinner Rolls

~

Pecan Pie

Barbecued Chicken

1 skinned chicken, cut into pieces
2 cups barbecue sauce of your choice
1 lime
1 garlic clove, pressed
1/2 cup canola margarine

Wash chicken parts thoroughly; pat dry. Place chicken parts in baking pan. Sprinkle pressed garlic, salt, and pepper sparsely over chicken and place margarine pats on each part. If cooking in the oven, place pan in 325° oven for 1 hour, basting frequently. If grilling, place a sheet of aluminum foil on white coal grill or medium grill. Place chicken on foil, cover and cook 45 minutes, turning and basting frequently. Coat chicken with barbecue sauce and continue basting frequently for 20 minutes more (10 minutes per side).

Barbecue Sauce the Healthy Way

2 tablespoons brown miso
1 tablespoon barley malt
1/4 teaspoon grated ginger
1/2 clove garlic
2 teaspoons oil

Blend all the above ingredients and refrigerate. Good for one month.

Green Salad of Your Choice with Papaya Salad Dressing

Pick your favorite greens from your garden or buy at the store. Decorate a large plate around the edges with greens. Leave an opening in the middle for the dressing for a beautiful presentation.

Papaya Salad Dressing

In blender, place 1 skinned and pitted papaya, tablespoon balsamic vinegar, a pinch of salt (optional), pinch of pepper, tablespoon of sesame oil. Blend for bumpy consistency and place mixture in middle of greens.

Double-cooked Mashed Potatoes

Make regular mashed potatoes from 4 potatoes mashed with 1 tablespoon canola margarine
4 oz. cream cheese
1/3 cup of extra milk
6 oz. mozzarella cheese
1/4 teaspoon black pepper

Make mashed potatoes and set aside. Melt cream cheese in milk until creamy. Add two mixtures together and put into casserole dish. Sprinkle with cheese and black pepper and bake until golden brown at 425°.

Quick Dinner Rolls

1-1/2 cups lukewarm water
1-1/2 tablespoon sugar
4 tablespoons canola oil
1/4 tablespoon salt
1 tablespoon yeast
1 egg
4 cups flour

In a small bowl, combine warm water, yeast, and 3 tablespoons canola oil. Stir and set aside on the TV or someplace warm for 8 minutes. In a large bowl, combine salt, sugar and eggs and cream together. Add yeast combination and mix. Slowly add flour and mix well. On a large cutting board, sprinkled with flour, knead the dough. Clean large bowl and grease it with 1 tablespoon canola oil. Return dough to bowl, cover and let rise back on warm surface for 20 minutes. Dough will double in size. Punch down and form dough into buns, then place into a greased pan. cover and let dough rise for 20 minutes more. Bake at 350° for 16 minutes or until golden brown. Cool on rack and serve with dinner.

Pecan Pie (see page 27)

German Fried Chicken

~

Rainbow Cole Slaw

~

Fresh Corn off the Cob

~

Broccoli au Gratin

~

Apple Crunch Pie

German Fried Chicken

1-1/2 pound frying chicken, cut up and skinned
2 eggs
1 cup barbecue sauce (see page 26)
1 cup corn flakes
1 cup flour
1-1/2 cups canola oil
Dash of salt and pepper

Wash chicken and pat dry. Mix eggs and barbecue sauce. Dip chicken in mixture and coat well. In a plastic bag, mix corn flakes, flour, salt, and pepper and shake chicken in bag. Heat oil and fry chicken 15 minutes on each side over medium heat.

Rainbow Cole Slaw (see page 52)

Fresh Corn Off the Cob

Cook corn. With a shearing knife, go up and down around cob removing kernels close to cob. Place kernels in bowl and dot with butter. Much nicer when having a romantic dinner than having to pick corn from your teeth after eating!

Broccoli au Gratin

1 head of broccoli
1/4 cup cream sauce

Steam broccoli. Make cream sauce using recipe on page 74. Pour sauce over broccoli and serve immediately.

Apple Crunch Pie

8 peeled and cored apples, sliced extra thin
2 tablespoons cinnamon
2 tablespoons brown sugar
1-1/2 cups fruit and nut, corn flakes cereal
3/4 cup canola margarine melted
1 teaspoon vanilla
1 egg

Heat oven to 375°. Lay apples in large cooking pan. In bowl, mix together sugars, margarine, eggs, and vanilla. Add cinnamon, brown sugar mix, and cereal in that order. Spread over apples and cook for 15 minutes. Serve with vanilla ice cream!

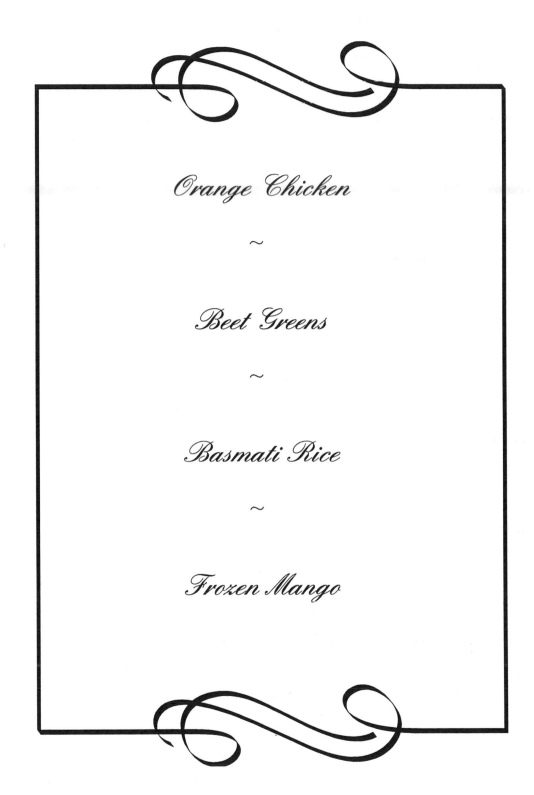

Orange Chicken

~

Beet Greens

~

Basmati Rice

~

Frozen Mango

Orange Chicken

1 chicken, whole or cut up
12 oz frozen orange juice, non-diluted
Salt and pepper to taste

Preheat oven to 425°. Wash chicken thoroughly and pat dry. Place chicken in pan and sprinkle with salt and pepper, inside and out. Cover chicken with orange juice. Cook 1-1/2 hours, basting often.

Beet Greens

This recipe is good to make when cooking beets.

1 bunch beet tops (greens)
3 tablespoons canola margarine
Pinch of garlic
Pinch of salt and pepper
1 teaspoon balsamic vinegar

While boiling water, cut tops off of fresh beets and lay beets aside. Wash the greens, pulling off any brown or old leaves. Drop the greens in boiling water for 3 minutes. Remove them and season with oil, garlic, salt, pepper, and vinegar. Season to taste. *They are unbelievably good!*

Try cooking the beets the same day to avoid extra cleanup. The natural red dye can be very messy, but well worth the time.

Basmati Rice (see page 34)

Frozen Mango (or other favorite fruit, such as papaya, berries, etc.)

Skin and pit mango. Cut into bite sized pieces and place on covered plastic plate in freezer for 12 or more hours. Serve as needed on plate and eat with toothpicks.

Place remainder in plastic bag in freezer and store for your next sweet tooth!

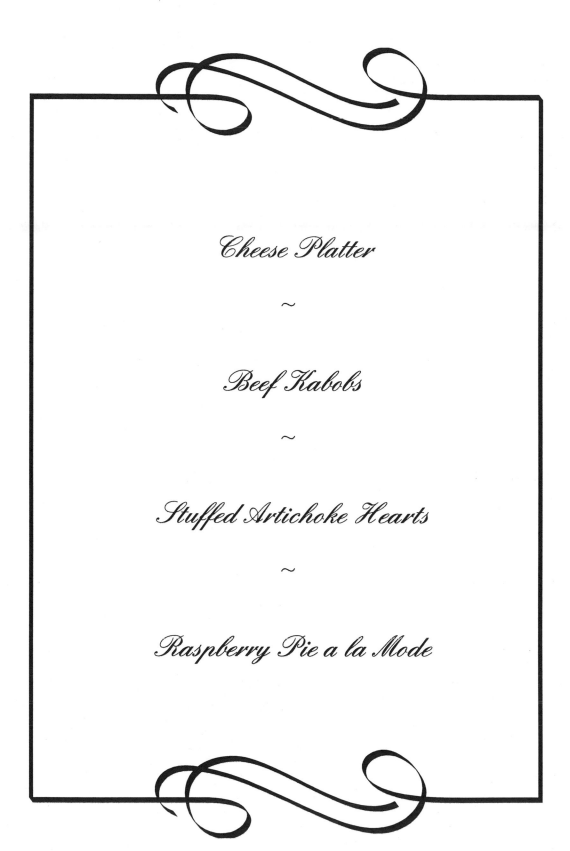

Cheese Platter

~

Beef Kabobs

~

Stuffed Artichoke Hearts

~

Raspberry Pie a la Mode

Beef Kabobs

1/2 cup canola oil
1/2 teaspoon rosemary
1 pound lean beef, cut into 1-inch cubes
1/2 cup chopped chives
2 large tomatoes, cut in wedges
8 ripe pitted olives
Salt and pepper to taste

Combine oil and seasonings. Add meat cubes and marinate overnight. Using four skewers, place meat, then vegetables, then olives on each skewer. Cook on medium heated grill for 7 minutes, turning evenly.

Cheese Platter

A small platter of your favorite cheeses is always nice. Try a variation such as the following:

Brie or camembert wheel with almonds. Press the almonds all over the cheese wheel and bake at 350° for 20 minutes. *What a treat!*

Stuffed Artichoke Hearts

1 large can artichoke hearts
1 8-oz package Philadelphia cream cheese, lite
1 small box Italian bread crumbs
4 large garlic cloves
1 cup Parmesan cheese, grated
1 cup olive oil to mix

Drain artichoke hearts and cut in thirds. Soften cream cheese and mix with all other ingredients. spread mixture on each piece of artichoke heart and serve.

Raspberry Pie a la Mode

4 cups fresh raspberries
1 cup corn starch
1 tablespoon canola margarine
2 tablespoons sugar
1/2 cup cold water
1 egg yolk

Graham Cracker Crust

1-1/2 cups graham cracker crumbs
1/2 cup canola margarine

Melt margarine in pie tin. Press graham cracker crumbs into margarine until pan is lined with moist mixture.

Preheat oven to 350°. In medium saucepan, combine sugar and corn starch. Gradually stir in water until smooth, then add egg yolk. Continue stirring constantly over medium heat until mixture starts to boil. Remove from heat and add margarine and fresh raspberries. Pour hot mixture into pie shell and bake for 25 minutes.

Zucchini Penne Italian Bake

~

Vegetable Platter

~

Pepper Bread

~

Orange Pie

Zucchini (or Eggplant) Penné Italian Bake

Penné noodles cooked and drained
Tomato sauce #2 (see page 43)
3 zucchini (or 1 eggplant)
1 cup Italian bread crumbs
2 beaten eggs
1 cup mozzarella cheese, shredded
1/4 cup Parmesan cheese
1 cup canola oil

Preheat oven to 450°. Slice zucchini (or eggplant) in 1/4 inch slices. Heat oil in frying pan. Dip slices in egg, then coat in bread crumbs. Fry each piece in canola oil until lightly brown on both sides. In pan, mix cooked noodles, tomato sauce, vegetable, Parmesan cheese and cover with mozzarella cheese. Bake for 40 minutes, covered. Turn broiler on and heat 10 more minutes to brown cheese.

Vegetable Platter

5 carrots
4 sprigs of celery
5 large radishes
1 green, yellow, and red pepper
5 florets of broccoli
5 florets of cauliflower

Wash and prepare all of above for steaming. Steam vegetables for 25 minutes. Place vegetables on a large platter with a bowl of dressing in the middle for dipping. You may also cut vegetables and serve raw in the same way.

Pepper Bread (see page 35)

Orange (or Lime or Lemon) Pie

1/4 cup fresh juice of desired fruit
1 rounded tablespoons canola margarine
1/2 cup sugar or substitute
1/4 cup corn starch
1-1/2 cups cold water
3 egg yolks, slightly beaten
3 egg whites
Grated peel of 1 orange, lemon, or lime
1 8-inch pie shell (see page 62)

Preheat oven to 350°. In medium saucepan, mix 1/2 of sugar with cornstarch. Gradually stir in cold water and stir until smooth. Next mix in the egg yolks. Over medium heat, bring to a boil while stirring constantly. Remove from heat and stir in margarine, grated peel, and juice. Spoon hot filling into crust. Beat egg whites with remaining sugar to form stiff peaks. Spread as topping and to seal crust. Bake for 20 minutes. Cool and refrigerate for 2 hours before serving.

Chapter Four: Autumn of the Heart

Cornish Game Hens with Wild Rice Stuffing
Deviled Asparagus
Popovers
Cranberry Medley
Chocolate Mousse

Rack of Lamb
Barbecue Sauce
Mixed Stuffed Vegetables
Green Chili Potatoes
Vanilla Cake with Maple Topping

Salmon with Cream Sauce
Sautéed Shitake Mushrooms
Eric's Skillet Potatoes
Cilantro Bread
Incredible Chocolate Raspberry Decadent Cake

Bonni and Frank's Turkey Dinner
Mung Bean Stuffing
Baked Acorn Squash
Fresh Corn on the Cob
Marshmallow Yam Casserole
Mashed Potatoes
Cranberry Medley
Sautéed Oyster Mushrooms
Chocolate Mousse Wedding Cake

Roast Duck
Vegetable Puree
Long Grain and Wild Rice, Hot or Chilled
Popovers with Honey Butter
Lemon Sorbet with Vanilla Ice Cream

Elegant Pizza with Pineapple and Tomato Sauce #1
Caesar Salad
Chocolate Mousse

Eggplant Parmesan with Provolone Cheese
Simple Salad with Healthy Italian Dressing
Turnip/Carrot Make Romance
Olive Loaf
Strawberry Rhubarb Pie

Cornish Game Hens with
Wild Rice Stuffing

~

Deviled Asparagus

~

Popovers

~

Cranberry Medley

~

Chocolate Mousse

Cornish Game Hens with Wild Rice Stuffing

The most romantic way to eat Cornish game hens is with the fingers, pulling apart the tender little pieces of succulent meat and feeding them to each other. Most of this meal—green sprigs of asparagus, steaming popovers—is best eaten without silverware, sucking the sauces and flavors from each other's fingers. Sit close and offer your lover the best pieces from your plate. You are sure to get your lover's best pieces in return. Serve the chocolate mousse from one bowl with two spoons, arms and tongues entwined.

2 Cornish game hens, washed and patted dry
Salt and pepper to taste
5 tablespoons butter
1/4 cup sliced water chestnuts
1/2 cup chopped mushrooms tops
2 tablespoons chopped chives
2 cups water
2 cups chicken broth
1 teaspoon lemon juice
1/3 cup uncooked rice
2 cups fruit compoté (see recipe below)

Season game hens with salt and pepper inside and out, then set aside.

In a small saucepan, melt 2 tablespoons butter, then sauté water chestnuts, mushrooms, and chives, stirring often, for 10 minutes. Add water, broth, lemon juice, and salt and pepper to taste. Bring mixture to a boil, then add rice. Reduce heat and cover, then simmer until water is absorbed, about 25 minutes.

Preheat oven to 400°. Lightly stuff game hens with rice mixture. Place birds in a shallow baking pan. Melt the remaining butter with the compote and brush on birds. Cover hens with foil and bake for 45 minutes, remove foil and bake for 30 minutes more.

Fruit Compoté
1-1/4 cups water
6 apricots or 3 peaches
1 tablespoon sugar
1 clove, crushed
Pinch of cinnamon

In a medium saucepan, bring water to a boil. Wash fruit, then place in boiling water. Lower to simmer and cook for 25 minutes. Remove fruit, reserving water, and set fruit aside. Place saucepan with water back on stove over medium heat. Add remaining ingredients and cook. Stir often until mixture is reduced by half, about 10 minutes.

Meanwhile, rinse fruit with cold water and remove peel by gently rubbing hands over fruit. Cut fruit in half and remove pits, then chop fruit.

When water spice mixture is reduced, add chopped fruit. Continue cooking and stirring until mixture thickens. Remove from stove.

Deviled Asparagus

1 tablespoon finely diced bell pepper
1 tablespoon finely chopped chives
1 tablespoon pimento
1 teaspoon Worcestershire sauce
1 can cream of mushroom soup
1 cup bread crumbs
2 tablespoons grated Romano or Parmesan cheese
1/4 cup melted butter
1 bunch asparagus, peeled and trimmed
5 tablespoons toasted almonds.

Preheat oven to 300°. Mix peppers, chives, pimento, and Worcestershire with soup. In a separate bowl, mix bread crumbs with grated cheese and melted butter. In a buttered casserole dish, pour in the soup mixture, then layer with asparagus. Spread bread crumb mixture over, then sprinkle with almonds. Bake for 30 minutes.

Popovers (see page 81)

Cranberry Medley

This recipe is so delicious we often eat it alone as a snack. In this menu, dip the meat and the popovers in and enjoy.

1 1-pound package fresh or frozen cranberries
1 cup diced pineapple
1/2 cup chopped walnuts
1 teaspoon sugar

Cook cranberries according to package directions. When cooled, mash one half with a potato masher. Mix with whole cranberries. Add remaining ingredients, mix well, and refrigerate for at least two hours.

Chocolate Mousse

1 4-ounce semi-sweet chocolate bar
2 tablespoons water
2 eggs, separated
Pinch of salt
1/3 cup sugar
1 cup whipping cream

Over low heat, melt chocolate with water, stirring constantly. Beat egg yolks well, then, stirring quickly, add to chocolate. Remove mixture from heat. Beat egg whites with salt, gradually adding sugar and beat to form stiff peaks. Fold egg whites into chocolate mixture. Whip cream and fold into chocolate mixture. Pour into serving bowl and chill overnight.

Rack of Lamb

~

Barbecue Sauce

~

Mixed Stuffed Vegetables

~

Green Chili Potatoes

~

Vanilla Cake with Maple Topping

Rack of Lamb

1 full slab of baby back prepared for grilling ribs, per person
1-1/2 cups of barbecue sauce of your choice
1 gallon water, boiling in large pot

Wash and pat ribs dry. Place 1 slab at a time into boiling water (unless you have a huge pot and can fill it with more water and therefore more ribs). Cook over medium-high heat for 20 minutes a slab. As you remove each slab, lay it out on a long pan and thinly coat with barbecue sauce. After all slabs are prepared for grilling, turn on grill and lay ribs out on grill, turning, basting, and cooking for 10 minutes each side of each slab. Add more barbecue sauce to taste.

Barbecue Sauce (see page 26)

Mixed Stuffed Vegetables

3 tomatoes
2 zucchini
2 eggplant
3 green peppers
1/4 cup chives, chopped
2 tablespoons butter
1 small clove garlic, minced
Pinch of oregano
Pinch of basil
1 egg (optional)
Bread crumbs (optional)
2 cups tomato sauce

Preheat oven to 375°. Cut tomatoes, zucchini, eggplant, green peppers, in half and scoop out pulp. Chop pulp and set aside. Steam green pepper and zucchini until tender. Sauté chives in butter until transparent and add garlic and vegetable pulp and herbs. If using, mix in egg and bread crumbs. Fill vegetable shells and place in casserole dish and cover with tomato sauce. Bake about 10 minutes or until green pepper is soft.

Green Chili Potatoes

3 russet potatoes, sliced long for French Fries
1 can chopped green chili peppers
3/4 cup grated mozzarella cheese
1 cup canola oil
2 tablespoons ketchup

Preheat oven to 425°. Make French fries by heating canola oil to 375° and frying potatoes.
After draining potatoes in drain basket or on paper towels, lay potatoes in baking pan. Sprinkle
green chili over potatoes, then cheese. Bake 20 minutes; serve with ketchup.

Vanilla Cake (see page 44) With Maple Topping

Maple Topping

1/3 cup margarine, softened
1/2 cup cocoa
8 oz. icing sugar
1/2 cup cold strong coffee

Using a mixer, cream margarine. Add cocoa, then alternately add cold coffee and icing
sugar. Beat until light and fluffy on medium-high speed.

Salmon with Cream Sauce

~

Sautéed Shitake Mushrooms

~

Eric's Skillet Potatoes

~

Cilantro Bread

~

*Incredible Chocolate Raspberry
Decadent Cake*

Salmon with Cream Sauce

1 salmon filet per person
Cream sauce recipe on page
1/4 cup canola oil

Preheat oven to broil. Wash and pat dry each filet. Brush with canola oil and lay fish in pan covered with foil. cook for 20 minutes or until tender. Prepare cream sauce while fish is cooking. When fish is done, lay one filet on each plate and cover with cream sauce.

Cream Sauce *(Good on just about anything romantic!)*

This sauce can be used on so many things. It's fast and easy to make. Just by changing the main herb, you can change the taste of it.

1 tablespoon canola margarine
2 tablespoons flour
1 chicken, beef, or vegetable bouillon cube (depending on your taste that evening)
1/8 teaspoon pepper
1 cup of milk
Pinch of each: dill, parsley, rosemary, plain or any dried herb in the dark green family

Cook your main item: VEGETABLES such as carrots or broccoli
FISH such as salmon filet
CHICKEN broiled, baked, or grilled
POTATOES skillet, baked, or fried

When your chosen dish is 6-7 minutes from being cooked, prepare sauce in heavy saucepan over medium heat. Combine flour, margarine, and pepper. Stir until all of the flour lumps disappear (about 1 minute). Add milk and herb, stirring constantly. In about 3-5 minutes, you'll have a thick delicious sauce ready to serve immediately.

Sautéed Shitake Mushrooms

1 pint fresh shitake (or oyster) mushrooms
3 tablespoons canola margarine
3 tablespoons chives
Salt and pepper to taste

Wash mushrooms thoroughly. Discard stems (all the purines settle in the stems and this is hard on your systems, especially for people with allergies). Slice the mushrooms as thinly as you like. Heat the margarine in a frying pan and lay mushrooms in pan. Sauté until slightly limp. Add other ingredients and cook for 3 minutes more. Serve.

***Note:** When buying button mushrooms, always look for mushrooms with caps fitting the stem tightly. Opening around the edges show an older product.

Eric's Skillet Potatoes

#1 russet potatoes
1/4 cup canola oil
Cheese of your choice (we like mozzarella)
Herbs of your choice (we like pepper, garlic, and jalapeño the best)

Peel potatoes and slice thinly. Place on a skillet in canola oil and turn heat to low. Cover and cook for 30 minutes or until browned on the edges, then put potatoes onto a microwavable plate and sprinkle with herbs and cheese. Cover the plate with plastic wrap and microwave for 1 minute on high. When cheese melts, serve and enjoy. They are delicious!

Cilantro Bread (see page 35)

Incredible Chocolate Raspberry Decadent Cake

9 ounces-semi sweet chocolate, finely chopped
1 cup (stick) salted butter
1-1/3 cups sugar
5 large eggs (blended)
Ganaché (see below)

With rack in center of oven, preheat to 325°. Melt chocolate with butter in top of double boiler with simmering water. Stir until smooth. Whisk in sugar. Continue to whisk 1-1/2 minutes. Whisk in eggs, then pour into a 9-inch spring form pan. Bake until the tester, which can be inserted into the center, comes out almost dry, but not wet (approximately 1-1/4 hours). Cool, then spread top with Ganaché.

Ganaché (Topping)

1/2 pound semi-sweet chocolate
1/2 cup half and half
1 pint raspberries

Melt chocolate with half and half in top of double boiler, stirring until smooth. Transfer to a shallow bowl. Let Ganaché stand at room temperature until cool. Spread with a knife around the sides of the pan. Invert onto platter. Remove bottom of pan. Spread 3/4 of the ganaché on top and sides, using the rest to decorate. Sprinkle raspberries on top. This dessert really is for 10-20 people, so you'll have great cake for a week if you're only a few people. Cutting down this recipe is too difficult, so enjoy it!!

Bonni & Frank's Turkey Dinner

~

Mung Bean Stuffing

~

Baked Acorn Squash

~

Fresh Corn on the Cob

~

Marshmallow Yam Casserole

~

Mashed Potatoes

~

Cranberry Medley

~

Sautéed Oyster Mushrooms

~

Chocolate Mousse Wedding Cake

Bonni & Frank's Turkey Dinner

1 12-pound turkey
Mung bean stuffing (enough to fill cavity of turkey)
3 tablespoons canola margarine
1 cup chives, chopped
1 can frozen orange juice
1 stalk carrot, chopped
1 stalk celery, chopped
1 cup chicken bouillon
Salt and pepper to taste

Mung Bean Stuffing

2 packages prepared stuffing mix
2 cups mung bean sprouts
1/2 cup chives, chopped
1/2 cup carrots, chopped
1/2 cup celery, chopped
1/2 cup canola oil
Sprinkle of salt and pepper
Sprinkle of thyme

Sauté chives, carrots, and celery in oil for 15 minutes. Add mung bean sprouts and spices and cook for 5 minutes more. Prepare stuffing mix according to mix directions and add sautéed items. Mix and set aside to be used for stuffing or side dish. (Leeks may be washed, cut, and steamed, then added to above stuffing for an incredible treat!)

Preheat oven to 350°. Fill turkey with stuffing and close cavities with skewers. Rub all over with canola margarine. Put vegetables and water in bottom of roasting pan. Sprinkle turkey with salt and pepper and pour frozen orange juice over turkey. Place on rack in roasting pan in oven for 3-1/2 hours, basting frequently with juices from bottom of roasting pan.

Baked Acorn Squash

2 acorn squash
1-1/2 cups honey
1/2 cup canola margarine
1 cup sherry (optional)

Cut squash in half. Scrape out seeds. Melt canola margarine and mix with honey and sherry. Fill each cavity. Bake at 357° for 1 hour.

Fresh Corn on the Cob

Marshmallow Yam Casserole

3 cups whole yams (drained and mashed)

1/4 cup brown sugar
1/2 teaspoon salt
1 teaspoon cinnamon
1 teaspoon nutmeg
1 tablespoon melted butter
1/4 cup cream
1-1/2 miniature recipe marshmallows

Blend yams with sugar, salt, cinnamon, nutmeg, melted butter, cream. Mix 1/2 marshmallows in baking dish. Grease top with remaining marshmallows. Bake at 320° for 20 minutes.

Mashed Potatoes

3 russet potatoes
3/4 cup of milk
2 rounded tablespoons canola margarine
Salt and pepper to taste

Cut and peel potatoes and place in rapidly boiling water with a little salt. Cook for about 20 minutes or steam them for about 30 minutes. Drain the water and add a pinch of salt and pepper to your taste, milk, and canola margarine. Mash until they are the consistency you like. *This potato recipe is very fattening so eat a small portion. Cheese may also be added for a delightful taste.*

Cranberry Medley (see page 68)

Sautéed Oyster Mushrooms (see page 74)

Chocolate Mousse Wedding Cake

Follow vanilla cake recipe on page 44, only make 4 times as much. Be sure to use 4 cooking pans. You can also go bigger if desired. Prepare cakes and cool. While cake is cooking, make 4 times the recipe on page 69 for chocolate mousse. When cakes are cooled, layer them with chocolate mousse recipe.

Meanwhile, pick your favorite topping from pages 44 or 72. When cakes with mousse filling are cool, spread frosting all over cake. Decorate with fresh flowers or a statue of a couple; or whatever means the most to the two of you.

Roast Duck

~

Vegetable Puree

~

Long Grain and Wild Rice,
Hot or Chilled

~

Popovers with Honey Butter

~

Lemon Sorbet with Vanilla Ice Cream

Roast Duck

1 duck cleaned, skinned, and oven ready
1/4 cup canola oil
8 oz. jar of peach preserves
1/4 cup low sodium soy sauce
1 tablespoon ginger
1/4 teaspoon salt
Dash of pepper
8 oz. of your favorite barbecue sauce

Preheat oven to 450°. Lay bird breast side down in broiler type pan (lots of holes in the top level for the grease to go through into the bottom pan). Sprinkle salt and pepper into the inside cavity of the bird. Brush canola oil over and around bird and set the bird aside. Meantime, mix all other ingredients.

Place bird on middle rack in hot oven and turn heat down to 425°. Cook for 1/2 hour. Brush 1/2 of peach mixture over top of bird. Turn bird over; brush other side again with canola oil and cook for 1/2 hour more. Remove bird from oven and discard grease from bottom pan. There's no more need for top part of broiler pan. Lay the bird in the bottom pan and cover completely with rest of peach preserve mixture. Cover the bird with aluminum foil and turn oven down to 350°. Let bird cook, basting regularly for 45 minutes more.

Vegetable Puree (see page 112)

Long Grain and Wild Rice, Hot or Chilled (see page 112)

Popovers with Honey Butter

1 cup flour
1 cup milk
1 egg
Speck of salt

Preheat oven to 425°. Put muffin tin in oven and let the tin turn sizzling hot.

Mix salt and flour. Add part of the milk slowly, stirring to form a smooth paste. Add the rest of the milk and well beaten egg. Cook for 1/2 hour, then turn oven off and let sit for 15 minutes more in the oven. Popovers will rise and be rather hollow. They should be split and eaten hot with butter and/or jam. Popovers can also be made with different herbs just by sprinkling your favorite herb into the batter. For a change, try adding a small amount of Parmesan cheese.

Honey Butter

1 cup soft canola margarine
1/2 cup clove honey

Put margarine into a medium sized mixing bowl. Take a large wooden spoon and spin mix the honey into the margarine. Put in serving dish with a cover and store in a cool place. Spread on your hot popovers.

Lemon Sorbet with Vanilla Ice Cream

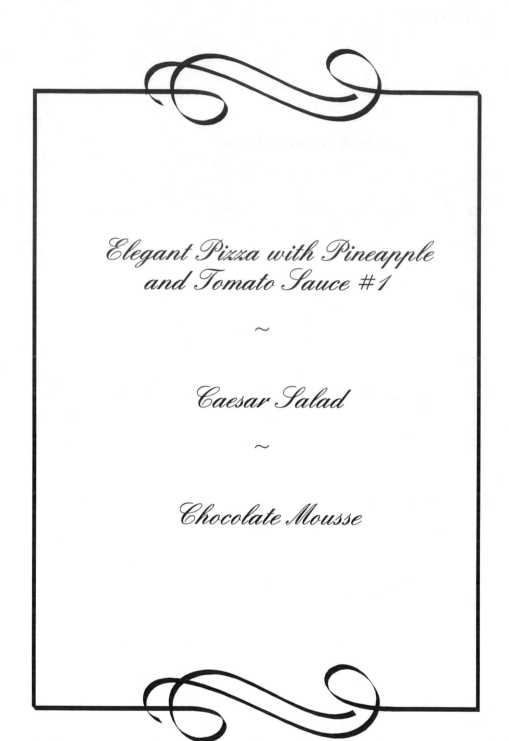

Elegant Pizza with Pineapple
and Tomato Sauce #1

~

Caesar Salad

~

Chocolate Mousse

Elegant Pizza with Pineapple & Tomato Sauce #1

Crust for pizza – store bought
Tomato Sauce #1
1-1/2 cups shredded mozzarella cheese
1 cup fresh pineapple cut into bite sized pieces
1/4 cup Parmesan cheese

Heat oven to 425° for 10 minutes. Lay crust right on oven rack. Cook for 5 minutes. Remove crust from oven and turn over crust. Place it on cookie sheet or foil. Smooth parmesan cheese and then tomato sauce on crust, then the mozzarella cheese and pineapple. Lay pizza back in oven and cook for 15 minutes more. Remove from oven and serve.

Tomato Sauce #1
3/4 cups of chives, minced
Garlic cloves, minced
1/3 cup canola oil
1/8 teaspoon cayenne pepper
1/4 cup chopped fresh anise
1/2 teaspoon each of ground oregano and crushed thyme
12-oz. can Italian style peeled, cooked tomatoes, chopped

Sauté chives and garlic in canola oil. Add all other ingredients. Simmer and cook for as many hours available to you that day, a minimum of 1-1/2 hours. The longer the sauce cooks, the fuller the flavor. If you only have an hour, you may need to add a little more salt to bring out the flavor.

Caesar Salad

1 cup water
1 egg (room temperature)
1/3 cup canola oil (olive oil may be used; in our experience the other flavors in this salad
    hold the true Italian flavor, so using a heavy oil is just added fat calories)
1-1/2 garlic cloves, halved; mince 1 clove
1 head Romaine lettuce, cut into bite sized pieces
1/4 cup grated Parmesan cheese (fresh, if you can find it)
1 tablespoon lemon juice
1 oz. anchovy fillets washed to remove excess salt and drained
Dash of pepper
1 cup of croutons

Hard boil the egg first. In a small sauce pan over high heat, heat water to boiling. Add egg in the shell and let stand for one minute. Remove and cool to room temperature. Combine lemon juice, anchovies, oil, minced garlic, and blend until creamy. Add peeled egg and blend for one more minute. Set aside for 2 hours. Now clean lettuce and dry. Break apart the head of lettuce by hand into bite sized pieces. Take bowl (wooden, if you have it) and rub other 1/2 of garlic clove around the inside of the bowl for flavor. Discard remaining garlic. Lay lettuce in bowl and sprinkle with Parmesan cheese and croutons. Coat with dressing mix and toss. ***Delicious!!***

Chocolate Mousse (see page 69)

Eggplant Parmesan with
Provolone Cheese

~

Simple Salad with Healthy
Italian Dressing

~

Turnip/Carrot Make Romance

~

Olive Loaf

~

Strawberry Rhubarb Pie

Eggplant Parmesan with Provolone Cheese

2 large mushrooms, cut in long cubes
1/4 cup canola margarine
4 oz. canned black olives chopped into small pieces
5 slices eggplant, 3/4 inch thick
1/4 pound provolone cheese, 1/8 inch thick
3/4 cup pine nuts
Tomato sauce #2 with lots of garlic (see page 43)

Preheat oven to 400°. Lightly sauté mushrooms in butter until limp (add 1 or 2 tablespoons water to keep heat down). Add olives and set aside. Have steamer pot going and steam eggplant until limp, about 3 minutes. Fill bottom of oiled glass baking dish with steamed eggplant; cover each slice with mushroom mix, then pine nuts, then cheese. Bake 5 minutes and serve with generous portion of tomato sauce.

Simple Salad with Healthy Italian Dressing

Eric suggested for a long time that I use cabbage instead of lettuce for salad. Chinese cabbage is a very delicate cabbage. It tastes as good and light as a Boston lettuce, and yet it is economical and healthier for you. Try it sometime—you won't be disappointed!

Large chunk of Chinese cabbage
1/4 cup grated carrots
1/4 sliced celery
1/4 cup grated mozzarella cheese
Dash of lemon
6 crackers of your choice

Slice cabbage into fine slivers. Add the other ingredients in any order. Then add any other vegetables you like. It tastes great once you toss it and add salad dressing. We like Ranch Lite or Low Fat Ranch dressings.

Healthy Italian Dressing

2/3 cup fresh lemon
2 tablespoons balsamic vinegar
2 tablespoons canola oil
1/2 pound Tofu
1 teaspoon tamari
1-1/2 teaspoons Dijon mustard
Dash of honey
1 tablespoon water
Dash of salt and pepper

Blend all ingredients together until creamy. Serve over a salad with one of my vegetarian recipes.

Turnip/Carrot Make Romance

1 large or 2 small turnips per person, peeled and cut into chunks
1 medium carrot per portion, peeled and cut into chunks
1 cup boiling water
1/4 cup milk
2 tablespoons canola margarine
Salt and pepper to taste

Heat turnips and carrots in water until soft, about 25 minutes. Remove from heat and drain excess water. With a potato masher, mash turnips and carrots together. Put back in pan over low heat and add other ingredients. Bring to the consistency you like and serve immediately.

Olive Loaf

Bread of your choice
Black or nicoise olives
Canola margarine

Take any of the breads you would use for herb bread. Split bread. Slice black olives thinly. Spread a little canola margarine on open loaves; sprinkle with a little mozzarella cheese. Cover cheese with olives and serve.

Strawberry Rhubarb Pie

3 tablespoons flour
1/4 cup sugar
2 cups fresh chopped rhubarb
1 cup sliced strawberries
1 egg, beaten
1/8 teaspoon salt
Pastry pie shell

Preheat oven to 425°. Place strawberries and rhubarb in shell. Whip egg, salt, sugar, and flour. Pour over rhubarb and top with lattice topped pastry. Bake for 10 minutes, then reduce heat to 325° and bake another 35 minutes.

Chapter 5: Warming Spirits In Winter

Bouillabaisse by the Fire
Sourdough Bread
Cheesecake with Strawberry Topping

Lentil Soup
Roast Crown of Pork
French Fried Russet Potatoes
Brussels Sprouts and Cauliflower
Apple Sliced Our Way with Cheese

Beluga Caviar
Filet Mignon
Our Favorite Potato Leek Soup
Tomato and Onion with Secret Sauce
Cheddar Cheese Popovers
Strawberry Shortcake

Stuffed Celery
Apple Sliced Your Way
Sushi Dinner
Bean Sprout Salad
Tofu Cheesecake

Mozzarella Cheese with Sun-Dried Tomatoes and Basil
Tuna Steak
Soothing and Steaming Broccoli
Cranberry Medley
Apple Pie

Chicken Cacciatore
Pasta Bowties
Dill Bread
Pistachio Blondies

Roast Rabbit
Green Chili Corn
Wild Rice Casserole
Vanilla Cake with Lemon Topping

Sage-Roasted Turkey Legs
Creamy Beets
Creamed Carrots
Potato Salad
Pecan Pie

Vegetable Puree
Long Grain and Wild Rice, Hot or Chilled
Spaghetti Squash Served with Tofu Meatballs
Millet Bread
Carrot Cake

Bouillabaisse by the Fire

~

Sourdough Bread

~

Cheesecake with Strawberry Topping

Bouillabaisse by the Fire

This meal does take some time and patience to prepare, but it is worth the effort. It is soothing on the palate and easy on the stomach, and very, very special. Make it on a chilly, house bound afternoon. Serve it in front of the fire, accompanied by a loaf of hot, crusty sourdough bread and butter. Finish off the meal with rich, luxurious cheesecake with strawberry topping.

Bouillabaisse

1 tablespoon butter
2 tablespoons olive oil
2 cup chopped chives
1/2 cup chopped celery
2 cloves garlic, finely minced
1/4 cup all-purpose flour
8 cups water
1 can (14-1/2 oz) whole tomatoes
1 cup dry white wine
2 tablespoons chopped parsley
2 tablespoons lemon juice
1 bay leaf
1/2 teaspoon salt
1/4 teaspoon cayenne pepper
1/4 teaspoon saffron
1 pound red snapper, boned skinned, and cut into bite-sized pieces
1 pound halibut fillets, boned, skinned, and cut into bite-sized pieces
1 pound raw shrimp, peeled
1 pint oysters
1 quart scrubbed clams in shells
1 whole Dungeness crab or a lobster in shell
1 whole crab, cleaned and broken into pieces
1/2 pound crabmeat

In a 6-quart kettle, melt butter and add olive oil. Lightly sauté the chives, celery and garlic until soft, not brown. Add the flour and stir until smooth. While stirring, slowly add water, tomatoes, wine, parsley, lemon juice, bay leaf, salt, cayenne pepper, saffron, and about 1/4 the snapper and halibut. Bring mixture to a boil and simmer for 20 minutes. Add the rest of the snapper and halibut and cook 6 minutes more. Add the shellfish and the crabmeat and cook another 5 minutes or until seafood is done. Taste and add more seasoning to taste.

Sourdough Bread - Fresh from your local bakery

Cheesecake with Strawberry Topping

1-1/2 cups whole almonds
1 cup oat flour
1/3 cup corn oil
1/4 teaspoon salt
2 8-oz. packages cream cheese
1/2 cup sugar
1/2 teaspoon vanilla
 2 eggs
1 cup sliced strawberries.

Preheat oven to 350°. Grind almonds into a meal using a food processor or coffee grinder. Mix almond meal with oat flour, corn oil, and salt. Press mixture into the bottom of an 8-inch spring form pan. Set aside. In a separate bowl, mix cream cheese, sugar, and vanilla until well blended. Add eggs and blend on medium speed for three minutes more. Carefully fold one half of the strawberries into the mix. Pour cream cheese mixture into crust, then top with remaining fruit. Bake for 40 minutes.

Lentil Soup

~

Roast Crown of Pork

~

French Fried Russet Potatoes

~

Brussels Sprouts and Cauliflower

~

Apple Sliced Our Way with Cheese

Lentil Soup (see page 25)

Roast Crown of Pork

1 crown of pork, oven ready
1-1/4 cups of fresh orange juice
1-1/2 tablespoons minced ginger
1 cup maple syrup
1-1/4 cups dry white wine
4 tablespoons dry mustard
1/3 cup soy sauce
3 tablespoons orange zest

Turn oven to 375°. Mix orange juice, ginger, maple syrup, wine, mustard, soy sauce, and orange zest; blend together. Coat pork and place in cooking pan. Roast for 20 minutes per pound. Baste pork often after the first half hour.

French Fried Russet Potatoes

3 russet potatoes (or yams)
1 cup canola oil
Ketchup for dipping

Clean, peel, and cut potatoes into sections for frying. Heat oil over medium high heat and lay potatoes gently into hot oil. Fry for 3 minutes or until brown. Ladle potatoes out of pan and lay on paper towels to drain.

Brussels Sprouts and Cauliflower (see page 26)

Apple Sliced Our Way with Cheese

I like to slice a whole apple, starting around the stem. Each slice will appear to have a star in the middle because you've cut right through the core of the apple. Slice the apple as thinly as you wish. Wash off any seeds that may be an eyesore. Serve with any of your favorite cheeses.
A wonderful dessert for any meal!

Beluga Caviar

~

Filet Mignon

~

Our Favorite Potato Leek Soup

~

Tomato and Onion with Secret Sauce

~

Cheddar Cheese Popovers

~

Strawberry Shortcake

Beluga Caviar

Every night may be a special night. For that special occasion: anniversary, birthday, a raise or bonus at work, try an ounce of Beluga Caviar. Get it fresh and serve it with a shell spoon or wooden spoon. Metal spoils the taste. Put it on a cracker or straight into your mouth. Caviar is a very sensual food. Try feeding each other a small spoonful at a time. Let the eggs sit on top of your tongue for a minute. Now burst them against the roof of your mouth. *Exquisite!!*

Filet Mignon

2 filet mignon steaks (1/2 lb. each allows for shrinkage)
1 tablespoon pepper
Salt and garlic to taste

Preheat broiler. Using drip broil pan, put 1-1/4 teaspoon pepper on the pan and place in oven for 5 minutes. When pan is hot, put steak on and sprinkle salt, pepper, and garlic to taste. Broil 5 minutes on each side and serve.

Our Favorite Potato Leek Soup

*Begin by buying 6 stalks of **fresh** leeks and 1 bunch of **fresh** chives. Leeks are especially good for women in keeping hormone levels healthy. The nutritional value is great; plus our men will love the taste. It almost seems to balance their levels too, because, unexplainably, whenever I serve this dish, my husband and I have the most romantic evenings after dinner.*

2 medium size potatoes
2 fresh stalks of leek
1/2 bunch of chives
1/3 cup of milk
1 large tablespoon flour
1 teaspoon canola margarine
Sprinkle of salt
Teaspoon of pepper

Cut in medium size pieces and soak leeks and chives for 10 minutes. They need to be well cleaned because dirt is collected especially between the leek leaves. Peel skin off potatoes and cut into bite-sized pieces. Once cleaned and cut, place leeks, chives, and potatoes in a medium size pot with a little bit more than just enough water to cover. Place cover on and heat until it boils, then simmer for 1-1/2 hours. While still on the heat, add milk, margarine, salt, and pepper. Stir until well blended. Add flour a little at a time, stirring with a large spoon quickly for the flour to dissolve. Serve with some homemade bread for an incredible meal!

Tomato and Onion with Secret Sauce

1 extra large tomato, cut into 1/8 inch slices
1 extra large Bermuda onion, cut into 1/8 inch slices

Lay tomatoes and onion slices alternating one then the other around the perimeter of the plate, saving one piece of each for the center of the plate.

Secret Sauce

1/2 cup barbecue sauce
1/8 cup balsamic vinegar
1-1/2 tablespoons canola oil
Dash of salt

Put all other ingredients in a container and shake well. Let each person put on their own amount of dressing. Serve dressing on the side in a gravy bowl with a spoon for serving.

Cheddar Cheese Popovers

2/3 cup flour
1/4 teaspoon salt
1/3 cup milk
1/3 cup water
2 eggs
1/3 cup shredded mozzarella or jack cheese
1/4 cup canola margarine

Heat oven to 425°. Put muffin tin in oven and heat the tin for 10 minutes. Meanwhile, mix flour and salt in a medium bowl. Add milk and water then mix. Beat in eggs. Fold in cheese. Place 1 tablespoon of margarine in each of the muffin circles and place back in oven for 4 minutes, until margarine melts. Now turn oven down to 375° and fill cups half full with batter. Bake until brown so they won't deflate, about 40 minutes. Serve with your favorite meal.

Strawberry Shortcake *(This is my husband's favorite!)*

1 angel food cake (store bought or any recipe will do. The following topping will make any angel cake taste divine!)

1 quart fresh strawberries
> Chop 3/4 of strawberries and put through the blender on low making a thick syrup
> Slice thin remainder of strawberries aside

1 pint of heavy cream for whipping
> Beat the cream on high until it becomes thick like whipped cream. You may add sugar; I don't.

1 thick gooey chocolate candy bar—sliced as thin as possible (optional)

Take the cooled angel food cake and slice carefully through the cake with a very sharp knife. The purpose being to make two symmetrical thinned down loaves. Take the bottom half and spread a thin layer of whipped cream on it. Then layer some of the thin sliced strawberries on top. This is where you can layer the candy bar if you've decided to use one. Put on the top half of the cake. Again layer with sliced strawberries and more whipped cream. At serving time, place the strawberry syrup separately on the table to pour over each slice served. Try using raspberries sometime for a deliciously different taste!

Stuffed Celery

~

Apple Sliced Your Way

~

Sushi Dinner

~

Bean Sprout Salad

~

Tofu Cheesecake

Stuffed Celery

Clean celery and lay out on a long platter. Fill the inside crease with whatever you have handy in the refrigerator, such as:

Creamed cheese
Left over fish, chopped finely with mayonnaise and chives
Peanut butter (ants on a log)

Be creative. Celery is a wonderful fiber food and great tasting, especially with a stuffing. Did you know that two stalks of celery a day will keep your bodily functions working?

Apple Sliced Your Way

Sometimes a light appetizer is nice. Take an apple and cut it up any way you like it. Try placing it in a pretty serving bowl or candy bowl. Sprinkle it with a little lemon juice to preserve the color. It's very delicious as well as being low in calories.

Sushi Dinner

This is one of our favorite dinners. Any gourmet or specialty store will carry Japanese products. If you have one, you can of course also go to your local oriental food store for some of these items. Placing chop sticks in the place setting will add to the mood of the evening. Feeding each other sushi with chopsticks gives a wonderful and romantic feeling. Wearing a Kimono will…as you wish it!

You'll need:

2 cups cooked Basmati rice
1 can Alaskan Red Sockeye Salmon
1 package seaweed
1 large sliced and steamed carrot
1 large yam, cooked and peeled
1 teaspoon wasabi (Japanese horseradish)
1/2 cup lite soy sauce
1/2 cup sweet pickled ginger
1 teaspoon sweet rice vinegar
1 package dried shrimp puffs
3 cups canola oil, heated until hot

Please note that this meal may be served on one large platter.

Prepare rice, using 4 cups of water to 2 cups of rice. Add 1 teaspoon sweet rice vinegar. Bring contents to a boil, then lower to simmer and cook rice until done, usually in 20 minutes. While rice is boiling, steam carrot and yam until soft. Mash them together and set aside. Open can of salmon and chunk apart. Mix wasabi in lumps and place on each end of the large platter. Pour soy sauce in small dish and set aside. Place about one teaspoon of sweet ginger per person in corner of platter on both ends of the serving plate. Lay sheets of seaweed along the counter, not overlapping. When the rice is prepared, place a 1-inch strip of rice onto the lower 1/3 part of each seaweed sheet. Then alternating, add salmon or vegetable onto rice/seaweed squares. Starting at bottom of square, roll up rice and filling to form log shapes. To seal the end of the log, dampen your finger with a tab of water. Run your finger along the open edge of the seaweed and press seaweed down lightly. The light water acts as a glue. When the edges are dry, take a very sharp knife and cut 1-inch sections along the logs, forming bite sized pieces. Lay out on platter with the filling side showing. Lay pieces onto the plate, together in clusters, Finish decorating the plate as you go along, by placing the ginger, wasabi, a sliced orange or parsley around the plate.

Heat oil. When hot, drop the flat dried shrimp circles in, using around 15 at a time. The shrimp pieces will immediately puff up. Remove them from oil and lay out on a paper towel to drain. Serve these with the sushi in a wicker lined basket. ***Enjoy!!***

Bean Sprout Salad

1/2 cup bean sprouts
2 tablespoons tahini
3 teaspoons sweet rice vinegar
1/4 cup sesame seeds
1/4 cup canola oil
Sprinkle of salt

Lay bean sprouts on individual salad plates in the middle of the plate, making an ant hill formation. Take other ingredients and shake in container, then sprinkle over each salad. Delicious when served with any oriental dish. If you feel the tahini is too heavy, try replacing the tahini with a barbecue sauce of your choice.

Tofu Cheesecake

3 cakes of tofu
3 tablespoons apple butter
1 cup apple juice
3 tablespoons ground rolled oats (ground in blender)
1/4 teaspoon salt
1 teaspoon vanilla
1 cup raisins cooked in 1 cup apple juice for 10 minutes, then pureed
1 8-oz. pie crust pg.

Preheat oven to 350°. Paint crust with apple butter 1/4" thick. Mix tofu, oats, salt, vanilla, and raisins well. Add puree and pour into crust. Bake 1/2 hour or until toothpick poked in center comes out clean. *Try using different fruit juices and decorating with pecan or other nuts.*

Mozzarella Cheese with Sun-Dried Tomatoes and Basil

~

Tuna Steak

~

Soothing and Steaming Broccoli

~

Cranberry Medley

~

Apple Pie

Mozzarella Cheese with Sun-Dried Tomatoes and Basil

This recipe takes 10 minutes to prepare and it's always in excellent taste in every way.

Fresh Buffalo or smoked mozzarella cheese cut into 1/8 inch slices or miniature mozzarella cheese balls

Sun-dried tomatoes (I like to put them in dry pressed olive oil with herbs. If you buy them totally dry, mix enough olive oil to cover the tomatoes and add whichever Italian herbs you like, such as basil, oregano, bay leaf, fresh ground pepper, etc., and soak until limp. Of course, you can substitute canola oil or even water; it may take longer to soak and the taste is lighter, and still delicious.)

Fresh basil; wash the basil well, then let it soak while you slice the mozzarella cheese.

Arrange the cheese on a pretty 10-inch plate, one next to the other or in a circle (not overlapping). Place 1 large or a few small fully dried leaves of basil on each slice of cheese; then place 1 large or a few small sun-dried tomatoes over the basil. The presentation is wonderful and the taste is superb!

Tuna Steak

2 1-inch thick tuna steaks
1 clove pressed garlic
1/4 cup soy sauce
1/4 cup canola oil

Mix all ingredients and marinate for at least one overnight. Broil or grill on foil over hot coals for 6 minutes per side.

Soothing and Steaming Broccoli

1 head of broccoli, cut into bite-sized pieces
2 tablespoons canola margarine
1 cup of water for steaming
juice of 1/2 lemon
Garlic to taste
Salt and pepper to taste

Place broccoli in boiling water or on steamer net. Cook until tender, about 12 minutes. Remove and place in bowl. Add margarine, then salt, garlic, pepper, and lemon juice. When under the weather, mash cooked mixture. Either way, it's just...*soothing.*

Cranberry Medley (see page 68)

Apple Pie

Crust of your choice
1 tablespoon flour
7 apples of your choice, peeled and cored and sliced thin
7/8 cup of sugar
1 teaspoon cinnamon
1/4 teaspoon allspice

Preheat oven to 450°. Stir spices with sugar, flour, cinnamon, and allspice. Pour mix in pie shell and bake for 10 minutes at 450°, then 30 minutes on 350°. Check every 5 minutes with a knife until apples feel soft. Remember to put foil under pie in the oven in case of spillage.

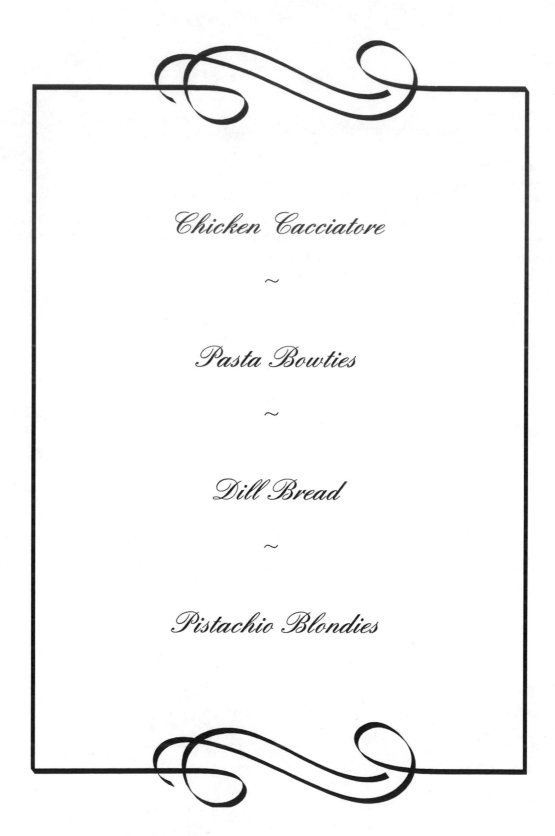

Chicken Cacciatore

~

Pasta Bowties

~

Dill Bread

~

Pistachio Blondies

Chicken Cacciatore

4 chicken legs and thighs
1 green pepper, chopped
1/2 cup canola oil
1/2 cup chives
1 large can of peeled whole tomatoes
1 cup sliced mushroom tops
1/2 cup sherry
1/2 teaspoon garlic
1/2 teaspoon oregano
1/8 teaspoon pepper
Undercooked spaghetti or pasta bowties

Brown chicken with chives and green pepper, frying chicken until almost done. Place chicken, spaghetti, spices, sherry, and vegetables in large casserole dish. Stir until combined. Bake at 350° for 1-1/2 hours.

Pasta Bowties

1 package pasta bowties, prepared according to package directions
Canola margarine
Salt, pepper, and garlic to taste

Mix cooked bow-ties, margarine, and spices, adding in that order. Serve as a side dish or a main course with steamed vegetables on top.

Dill Bread (see page 35)

Pistachio Blondies

1 cup pistachio nuts, whole
1/2 cup pistachio nuts, chopped
3/4 cup canola margarine
1/2 cup brown sugar
2 tablespoons white sugar or substitute
2 eggs
2 cups flour
1 teaspoon baking soda
1/2 teaspoon salt
1-2/3 cups toffee chips

Heat oven to 350°. Grease baking pan. In large bowl, beat butter and sugars until fluffy. Add eggs and blend well. In small bowl, mix flour, baking soda, and salt and gradually add into butter mixture. Mix well. Stir in toffee chips. Spread in prepared pan and bake for 35 minutes or until golden brown. Cool completely before cutting.

Roast Rabbit

~

Green Chili Corn

~

Wild Rice Casserole

~

Vanilla Cake with Lemon Topping

Roast Rabbit

2 teaspoons salt
2 teaspoons black pepper
1 tablespoon canola oil
1 rabbit, oven prepared, cut into 5 pieces
3 tablespoons rosemary

Preheat oven to 375°. Place the rosemary in a large roasting pan and toss with salt and pepper and canola oil. Rub mixture thoroughly over and inside of each piece of rabbit. Place the rabbit in the oven and roast for 40 minutes. Turn pieces over and baste well. Cook for 15 minutes more and serve.

Green Chili Corn

1 small can of green chili peppers, diced
3 to 5 ears of corn
1 tablespoon canola margarine
Dash of pepper

Remove kernels from ears of corn and put in pan with other ingredients. Steam in margarine for 10 minutes and serve.

Wild Rice Casserole

1/2 cup uncooked wild rice
1/2 cup canola margarine
1/2 cup mushroom tops, sliced
2 tablespoons chopped chives
2 tablespoons minced green pepper
1/2 clove garlic, minced
1-1/2 cups chicken broth
Pepper to taste (optional)

Preheat oven to 325°. Wash rice and soak overnight, then cook rice in hot steamy water for one hour. Melt margarine and add mushrooms, chives, green pepper, and garlic. Cook 7 minutes, stirring often. Drain rice and add to mushroom mixture. Add broth and pepper. Pour into a greased casserole dish. Cover and bake for 1 hour, then uncover and continue baking 25 minutes more or until all the liquid is absorbed.

Vanilla Cake (see page 44) with Lemon Topping

Lemon Topping

1-1/2 cups icing sugar
1/3 cup canola margarine, softened
1/4 cup lemon juice
1 teaspoon grated lemon rind
1-1/2 teaspoons vanilla

Using a mixer, cream butter; add lemon rind. Alternately add lemon juice and icing sugar. Beat on medium-high speed until light and fluffy. Add vanilla and mix 1 minute more.

Sage-Roasted Turkey Legs

~

Creamy Beets

~

Creamed Carrots

~

Potato Salad

~

Pecan Pie

Sage-Roasted Turkey Legs

2 turkey legs
1/2 cup canola oil
1/4 cup chopped chives
2 cups thinly sliced mushrooms
8 sage leaves
Sprinkle of salt and pepper

Preheat oven to 400°. Heat oil in a large skillet over medium heat. Add the mushrooms and chives and sauté until browned and softened, about 5 minutes. Place 4 sage leaves under each turkey leg. Pour mushroom mix over turkey legs and heat about 40 minutes in the oven, basting and turning frequently.

Creamy Beets

1 bunch of beets
1 tablespoon onion, grated (optional)
1/2 cup sour cream
Salt and pepper to taste

I prepare these the same day I cook the greens, due to the clean up factor being somewhat timely. Use the boiled water from the greens and cook beets in simmered water until tender, usually 45 minutes, and drain. Cool completely in refrigerator. When completely cooled, stir in salt, pepper, and sour cream and grated onion, if using it. Refrigerate again for 1/2 hour before serving.

Creamed Carrots

2 to 3 large carrots, peeled
1-1/2 tablespoons canola margarine
3 tablespoons flour
1 chicken bouillon cube
1/8 teaspoon pepper
1 cup milk
Sprinkle of dill

Slice carrots. Cook until tender and drain. While carrots are cooking, prepare the sauce in a heavy saucepan over medium heat. Combine flour, margarine, and pepper and stir out all flour lumps. Add milk, bouillon cube, and dill, stirring constantly until thickened (if still liquidy, add a touch more flour). Pour over cooked carrots and serve.

Potato Salad

1 cup low fat mayonnaise
4 hard boiled eggs, coarsely chopped
12 small to medium red potatoes, well boiled and coarsely chopped
3 sweet gherkins, chopped
3 tablespoons gherkin pickle juice
1/3 cup chopped celery
1/3 cup chopped greed pepper
1/3 cup chopped chives
1/4 cup chopped parsley
1 tablespoon mustard for color
Dash of garlic
Dash of pepper
Dash of paprika

Mix mayonnaise, 3 eggs, potatoes, pickles, pickle juice, celery, green peppers, chives, parsley, mustard, garlic, and pepper. Slice the 4th egg for decoration, then sprinkle paprika over the top.

Pecan Pie (see page 27)

Vegetable Puree

~

*Long Grain and Wild Rice,
Hot or Chilled*

~

*Spaghetti Squash Served
with Tofu Meatballs*

~

Millet Bread

~

Carrot Cake

Vegetable Puree

3 cups celery root
2 medium sized baking potatoes
2 medium turnips
4 medium leeks (white part only)
1 tablespoon salt
Pepper to taste

Place celery root, potatoes, turnips, and leeks in a large saucepan and cover with cold water. Place over medium-high heat and bring to a boil, then lower heat and simmer about 30 minutes or until vegetables are all tender. Puree in a blender or a food processor.

Long Grain and Wild Rice, Hot or Chilled

1/2 cup wild rice
1 cup long grain rice
3 cups water
Pinch of salt

Clean and soak rice overnight. Then add above ingredients together and boil. Cover and turn heat down. Simmer for 35 minutes or until water is absorbed.

Spaghetti Squash Served with Tofu Meatballs

Meatballs

1 pound tofu
1/4 cup bread crumbs
1/2 cup chives, chopped
1/2 cup chopped green peppers
1 bunch parsley, chopped
1 tablespoon margarine
1 egg
1 tablespoon tomato sauce (see page 43)
Dash of Oregano, basil, and marjoram

Mix above ingredients and form meatballs. Roll in flour and place on well-oiled cookie sheet. Bake until golden brown, about 1 hour.

Spaghetti Squash

Cut squash in half, scoop out seeds. Bake on cookie sheet, hollow side down, in 1/4 inch of water. Bake at 350° for 1 hour. Using a fork, peel squash from shell (it comes out like spaghetti). Serve with tomato sauce and Tofu meatballs.

Millet Bread

2 cups millet, ground until flour consistency
1/2 teaspoon baking soda
2 eggs
1/2 cup olive oil
1/2 cup clover honey or molasses
1/2 cup walnuts or almonds, half chopped, half whole
2 cups very ripe banana
12-inch baking loaf pan

Preheat oven to 350°. Take millet and baking soda and mix in a small bowl and set aside. Take eggs, olive oil, honey or molasses and mix in a separate small bowl, then set aside. Mash the bananas in a large bowl. Now add the millet mixture to the banana, then add egg mixture. Slowly add in the chopped nuts and stir. Put into baking loaf pan and decorate with left over whole nuts on top. Bake at 350° for 30 minutes, or until done. Test doneness by sticking a toothpick through the middle; it should come out clean when done.

Carrot Cake

1-1/2 cup raisins (optional)
3 cups carrots, grated
1-1/2 cups coconut (optional)
1-1/2 cups mashed walnuts or mixed nuts, mashed
1/2 teaspoon baking soda
1-1/2 cups canola oil
1 cup brown sugar
1-1/2 cups whole wheat flour
4 eggs
1/2 teaspoon cinnamon
Pinch of salt

Blend oil and eggs in a small bowl. Mix all other ingredients in large bowl, then add egg mixture. Pour mixture into pan and bake at 300° for 1./2 hour or until done.

Frosting

1 8-oz. cream cheese
1 powdered white sugar or honey and sugar mixed
1 teaspoon vanilla
1/3 stick butter

Mix together and frost cooled carrot cake.

Appendix:

Mealtime Savers

~

Stain Removers

~

Weights & Measures

Mealtime Savers

R$_X$ before you cook:

Boiling a Mixture: Generally when boiling a mixture, bubbles will break the surface at boiling point. I usually suggest never to boil anything but water for tea. Boiling usually breaks a mixture and clouds your food. What I suggest is to stand by your stove when boiling food. Just as you start to see the first slight bubble, turn your mixture to low and simmer it slowly. Sometimes I remove the pot for a minute to let the cooking cycle slow down.

To Sauté Food: Put a small amount of oil (use canola or olive because they are most easily assimilated when hot) in a pan. Turn to medium heat and let the pan heat up for a few minutes. To test the oil, drop a morsel of food into the pan. If the food hops, the oil is ready. You don't want to let food sit in grease or oil—not ever. It makes food heavy and limp. You constantly stir your food around once it is in the pan.

Braising Food: This is good for cooking tough meat. Rub the meat with a small amount of oil. Place the meat in a hot oven, 450°. After the meat browns, usually about 10 minutes, lower cooking temperature to 250°. The meat will cook very slowly and will be succulent when finished.

Some Helpful Ideas on Bread:

To Thaw: To thaw frozen bread loaves, place them in a clean brown paper bag and lay in the oven at 325° for about 5 minutes or until completely thawed. Rolls take 12 minutes. If using the microwave, 15 seconds should suffice.

Active Yeast: Add 1/2 teaspoon of sugar to yeast when stirring it into the water to dissolve. If it foams and bubbles in ten minutes, you know the yeast is active.

Bread Dough that Doesn't Rise: Set dough on heating pad for a few minutes. Another way is to turn on the television and lay dough on top of it. The heat from the TV works wonderfully.

Stale Bread into Bread Crumbs: Stale whole wheat, rye, white, or sourdough may be slowly dried in the oven until brittle, then put away in a container for breading foods. Larger pieces of stale bread may be cut into thin squares and used in place of crackers for soups and croutons.

To make Stale Bread Soft: Stale bread, rolls, or muffins may be sprinkled slightly with 1/2 teaspoon of water and then toasted for 3 minutes or microwaved for 30 seconds to bring softness back into the bread.

Crispness: To make your bread crusty, brush sides and top of your bread with an egg white that has been beaten with one tablespoon of water.

Moist Bread Dough: Use water that has been used to boil potatoes.

Sogginess: Let bread stand on a cool wire rack to avoid sogginess.

Steadiness: While making bread, place a folded, damp towel under the bowl to prevent slipping and sliding while you are mixing.

Sticky Hands: To avoid sticky hands, knead dough in a large plastic bag.

Remember: Keep a biscuit mix on hand to stretch a dinner in case extra guests arrive. Biscuits are a good filler to any meal.

Seafood

Shellfish: Before opening clams, oysters, fresh shrimp, and other shellfish, brush clean with a solution of baking soda and water.

Storage: Always store any fish in a cold place until ready for use. If not using right away, freeze it.

Firmness: To make fish firm in Bouillabaisse, add a little lemon juice to soup while first boiling.

Odors: To avoid odors, cover fish with a little browned butter and lemon juice.

Sticking: To keep fish from sticking, bake fish on a bed of celery and onion. This also enhances the flavor.

Chicken

Flouring: Chicken may be floured by placing flour and dry spices into a plastic bag and adding the meat, then shake well.

Handling: Please be wise when handling chicken. Of all the meat products on the market, many chickens contain the highest bacteria. Of course, for those of you lucky enough to raise chickens on your own property or buy from a friend, you know how long a chicken has been sitting out after slaughter. We eat chicken every week, but for now we're buying at an organic chicken farm. These farms are using less abusive procedures in raising chickens. Chickens are fattened up with soy at these farms. One day, we hope to raise our own.

Date Stamp: If the expiration date is less than 5 days away, ***Don't buy that chicken!*** Be aware that some markets are not current and may actually repackage chicken in order to sell more. If possible, go to the fresh meat section of the market and pick out what you want there. It doesn't cost anymore, and you'll be sure the chicken is fresher.

Usage: If not using the chicken the day it comes from the market, freeze it until needed. Don't freeze it for more than 3 months because even the freezer won't stop that high bacterial growth from happening.

Preparation: When preparing, always wash chicken thoroughly. We never use the skin because of the bacteria. Skin the chicken and cook it wrapped in foil or in a pan covered with foil. We use a clay pot, which keeps the skinned chicken moist. You can also fry skinned chicken. Refrigerate first for one hour and the batter will stick better. Simply make the batter of flour, salt, and pepper. dip the chicken in milk first, then shake in a bag with the batter ingredients.

Cooking Chicken: Cook chicken breast side down to keep the white meat moist. If your chicken comes out dry, make a sauce of equal parts butter and chicken broth or stock. Pour mixture on the sliced bird and let stand in a 250° oven for 10 minutes or until all the juices are soaked up.

Odors: Rub poultry with salt and lemon juice to lessen any unpleasant odors.

Notes: Short legs and plump breast indicate a fuller white meat section.
Black feet on a turkey indicate a young bird. A short turkey within 8-10 pounds is the best buy because it has more white meat and less carcass in proportion than a larger bird.

Meat

Tough Meat: Tough meat requires a different treatment from tender meat. Both should be cooked in consideration of retaining the juices. A tender cut should be cooked at a higher temperature than tougher pieces.

Bone Marrow: can be used to nourish a dish such as a meat stew.

Grease: For less grease, sprinkle salt in the frying pan before adding meat.

Juicier Meat: For a juicier burger or meatloaf, rub both sides with cold water before grilling.

Carving: A large roast can be carved more easily if you let it stand for 20 minutes before carving.

Cleanup: For easier cleanup, add cold water to the bottom of the broiling pan before cooking meat. The water will absorb the smoke and grease.

Gravy: When making gravy, pour the pan drippings into a tall jar. The grease will rise to the top in minutes and can be easily removed.

Flouring: Meat may be floured by placing flour and dry spices into a plastic bag and adding the meat; shake well.

Leftovers: Chop up and add to corn chips. Then top with beans, cheese, green chilies, cheese, and anything else you like for a fantastic nacho snack or meal.

Frying: When frying meats, let meat sit in a bowl of milk for 24 hours in the refrigerator. You'll find the meat is tender and much tastier.

Vegetables

Vegetarian dishes are handy to prepare. We grow many of our own vegetables. With so many new chemicals being sprayed these days, we are uncomfortable not knowing the handling of the food we buy. Because of the nutritional value, however, we suggest eating as much in the vegetable food group as possible. Vegetables supply the nutrients and roughage required for the body to function properly.

Pretty easy equation of life to follow: Good food = good bodily functions = more love at home. It's worth it to us to put aside sweets and greasy food for that feeling at home!

Vegetables may be steamed or raw. Please remember to chew raw vegetables well for better assimilation.

Overcooked vegetables may be sliced or mashed with any creamed soup.

Cold vegetables that go limp can be frozen for 20 minutes or until they firm up.

Asparagus: Stalks should be tender and firm; tips should be close and compact. Stalks with very little white are more tender. Use them within 3 days, before they start to toughen.

Broccoli, Brussels Sprouts, and Cauliflower: These flower cluster vegetables are delicious. When buying, look for flower clusters that are tight and close together. Brussels sprouts with smudgy dirty spots may indicate insects. Look your vegetables over carefully. These flower cluster vegetables may be cooked in so many different ways. Our favorite is to steam them over a pot of boiling water for 10 minutes. Dot with canola margarine, and a touch of garlic and pepper.

Cabbage and Head Lettuce: Heavy head sizes are the best. Avoid cabbage with worm holes and avoid lettuce with discoloration or soft rot.

Cucumbers: Long and slender cucumbers are the best tasting; Don't buy one with yellowing parts.

Peas and Lima Beans: Select pods well-filled, but not bulging. Avoid dried, spotted, yellowed, or flabby pods.

Scallions: Scallions are good to add flavor to any bland meal. Many people allergic to regular onions can eat scallions instead. Scallions don't have as strong a flavor as the regular onion does.

Root Vegetables: As a rule, root vegetables should be smooth and firm.

> **Carrots:** Carrots may have woody cores. Fresh carrot tops usually indicate fresh carrots. Conditions of leaves on most other root vegetables do not indicate the degree of freshness.

> **Turnips, Beets, and Parsnips:** Keep a medium size. Oversized are fun to look at, but they may be woody.

> **Radishes:** Oversized radishes may be pithy. Buy a medium size when possible.

> **Potatoes:**

> **NOTES:** Remember to wash skins well, especially if you're planning to eat the skins. When growing potatoes, a lot of chemicals are sometimes placed in the soil. That is because of how sensitive potatoes are to bugs in the ground. So you want to soak those chemicals off as much as possible before eating the skin. The skin can be quite delicious.

> For years, retailers have interchanged the names for sweet potatoes and yams. Sweet potatoes range in color from yellow to deep orange. They grow well in many southern states and in tropical environments. They are shaped like a turnip and bruise easily. Yams are white, ivory, or yellow. They grow very large and are mostly seen in Western Africa. What is most often sold in the supermarket is the sweet potato, very often misnamed the yam.

> **Sweet Potatoes:** The bronze skins are soft and sweet when cooked. Yellow to light brown ones are firmer and less moist.

> **Fuller Tasting Potatoes:** Sprinkle potatoes lightly with flour before frying for a fuller taste and toasty color. You can also add seasoning to the flour before coating.

> **Leftovers:** Cut into small pieces. Put in saucepan with 3/4 cup low fat or lactaid milk, 2 tablespoons canola margarine and season to taste while steaming mixture over medium-low heat. Sometimes I'll steam leeks and scallions to add to mixture for a delicious potato-leek combination soup!

Rice and Pasta

When preparing pasta, add vegetable oil to pasta water to cut down on sticking. Rub shortening around the top of the pot to prevent boiling over. An easy to cook pasta is to bring salted water to a boil, stir in pasta, cover, and turn off the heat. Check the pot in about 10 minutes for a well-done pasta!

Pasta that Is Sticking: Plunge your cooked pasta into boiling water with olive oil and gently separate with a large fork.

Burned Rice: Take the pot off the stove and put a heel of a loaf of bread on top of the rice. Cover the pot and wait 8 minutes. Taste the rice and decide for yourself whether or not to serve it.

Rice that May Stick: A teaspoon of lemon juice to each quart of water will keep the rice white and separated.

Fruits

Melons:

> **Watermelons:** They may be ripe and still have some yellow color on one side. White or pale green on one side indicates they are not yet ripe.

> **Cantaloupes:** Thick close netting on the rind indicates the best quality. When the stem scar is smooth and space between the netting is yellow or yellow-green, they are ripe. When you smell the fruity odor, they are the best.

> **Honeydews:** They are ripe when the rind has a creamy to yellowish color and velvety texture. Immature honeydews are whitish-green.

Oranges, Grapefruit, and Lemons: The heavier the better. Smoother, thinner skins usually indicate more juice. Most skin markings do not affect quality. Oranges with a slight greenish tinge may be just as ripe as fully colored ones. Light or greenish-yellow lemons are more tart than that of deeper yellow ones. Avoid citrus fruits showing withered, sunken, or soft areas.

Frozen Peaches: Keep frozen peaches on hand. They are great in emergencies. Garnish a skimpy salad, or fix a dry cake. Put the peaches into a blender and mix with a tablespoon of water to make a peach sauce. They can also be used when cooking any fish or poultry for special flavor or to prevent dryness.

Skin Removal: To remove the skins of peaches or apricots, prepare a solution of 1/2 cup baking soda and 2 gallons of water. Bring the water solution to a boil; drop fruit in and skin will loosen easily after a short time. Take the fruit to the sink and rinse under cold water to make removal easier.

Berries: Plump, solid berries with strong family color are best. Avoid stained containers which indicate wet or leaky berries from the market.

Lemon Juice: Add 1 teaspoon to each quart of water for a refreshing drink, or use on fish to block any odor. You can also add to rice to keep the rice white and separated.

Cheese

- Rub grater with oil before grating cheese for an easier cleanup.
- Use a dull warm knife for slicing cheese.
- Soak hardened cheese in buttermilk to soften.
- Storing cheese in a tightly covered container with a few sugar cubes will retard mold.

Eggs

Egg Whites: Two egg whites may be substituted for each egg needed in a recipe. This may help you with dietary limitations.

Batter: When making a batter, eggs should be beaten first and then slowly added to your batter. This will keep the batter from getting too heavy.

Cracked Eggs: Cracked eggs need not be thrown away. Use them in cakes or custards at once.

Yolks: Egg yolks can be kept for several days in the refrigerator if covered with vegetable oil.

Desserts

Melting Chocolate: To melt chocolate, use a double boiler if available. Bottom pan has 1 inch of simmering water. In top pan, break chocolate into small pieces and stir constantly. If only one pan is available, break pieces and melt slowly over very low heat. Remove from heat as soon as chocolate melts to avoid burning.

Meringue: When making meringue, turn off the oven just as the meringue turns brown. Leave the door open slightly and the pie will cool slowly preventing the meringue from splitting.

Pudding: Any pudding can be used for making a quick pie filling. Vanilla or chocolate instant pudding will camouflage unattractive desserts. I once made a dry white cake and ended up slicing or chunking the cake. When topped with pudding, it still needed something else so I defrosted peach slices and added those to the top of the dessert. It was a great success!

Dry Pies: To eliminate dryness, brush frozen pies with melted butter before baking.

Pie Crust: If a pie crust browns to fast, cover the pie with a sheet of foil after 15 minutes of cooking time. Make sure you preheat the oven for 15 minutes before cooking so that the coils aren't too red hot in your oven.

Frosting: When frosting a cake, first apply a sprinkling on top of each layer. This will keep the filling from soaking through the cake.

Frosting: When frosting a cake, start with a thin layer of frosting. This will keep the filling from soaking through the cake. Then, set it aside for 30 minutes. Apply the second coat later for a smoother, more professional looking cake.

Fresh or Frozen Peaches: Keep these in your home for an emergency. They're good on any dessert or alone for a last minute dessert.

Frozen Fruits: Skin and freeze papaya or mango or melon for a great dessert. Fresh berries or grapes put in plastic bags are delicious for a mid-afternoon snack.

R_x for Problem Desserts

Cakes that don't Rise: Rename them! They still taste good. Make a pudding and place inside your sliced cake. *Or* cut and place fruit and whipped cream in the middle of your cake. If the presentation still looks bad, frost it!

Burned Edges, Soupy Middle: Finish baking the cake, then cut off the burned edges. Now garnish as you like. Use some of the decorating ideas from the suggestions above on *Cakes that don't Rise*.

Dry Cake: Wrap the cake in cheesecloth that has been soaked in blackberry brandy. Let sit for 10 minutes and discard cheesecloth. Then top with whipped cream and berries in season.

Bland Cake or Cookies: Turn bland cookies into sandwich cookies or cake using creams, jams, or fudge!

Stale Cake: Stale cake makes a good cottage pudding. Cut away all the frosting from the cake and arrange in slices on individual plates, then pour hot lemon sauce over it. Top with a bit of jelly.

To Thicken Foods: To ensure a perfect thickening such as for gravy, use a whisk or a hand beater. Stir your thickener in slowly and you'll rarely have problems with that dish. If you do by some chance totally mess up your meat or poultry gravy, you can take a bullion cube or 2, dissolve it in hot water, and slowly add your thickener again. Your gravy will taste as good as the original meat gravy and doesn't have the fat.

Bullion cubes are good to have on hand for that one time you have company and spoil the first gravy mix.

Baking Soda may be used in the gravy, 1/2 teaspoon at a time, to decrease excess grease. It will not affect the taste of the gravy.

Corn Starch or Flour: Both corn starch or flour can be used as above to thicken hot foods.

Note: To thicken a runny pie, remember that for every six cups of fruit, use 1-1/2 tablespoons of cornstarch or 3 to 4 tablespoons of flour. If a fruit is extra runny, add more cornstarch or flour after 5 minutes of stirring. Too much of anything is no good, so be patient when adding extra thickening because the mixture will sometimes thicken too much and taste pasty.

Agar-Agar: Agar-agar is a seaweed-based vegetable. It is used to thicken all kinds of food, hot or cold. It is found in all natural food stores, and in some super markets. You can take any liquid, such as juice, soup, water, broth, let cool and stir 2 tablespoons of Agar-agar to start into the liquid. In a few minutes, it will thicken. Add a little more after 2 minutes of stirring if needed. Agar-agar has no taste and takes on whatever flavor you are cooking as it cooks into that dish.

Oatmeal: May be used to thicken soup and add good nutritional value at the same time.

To Ensure a Fresh and Tasty Meal, Remember:

- The coldest part of any refrigerator is the back of the top shelf.
- Every cubic foot of the freezer is capable of freezing no more than four pounds of fresh food at one time.
- Every time you open the oven door, the temperature drops about 20 degrees.
- Wrap lettuce in paper toweling to prevent discoloration.

Food that is too Salty: Add a cut raw potato. Once the food is prepared, throw the potato away.

Food that is too Sugary: Add salt, or if it is a main dish, add vinegar.

Food that is too Sharp: A teaspoon of sugar will soften the taste.

Stain Removers

Coffee: Soak or sponge the area with water right away, then wash the garment as soon as possible, using detergent and bleach which is safe for fabric.

Grease: Use non-flammable dry cleaning solvent. Let sit for 20 minutes, then wash the garment with detergent and bleach which is safe for fabric, then wash again.

Chewing Gum: Rub the area with ice. After 20 minutes, scrape the area with a dull blade. sponge the garment with dry cleaning solvent and air dry. Wash in hot water with detergent.

Alcoholic Beverages: Presoak fresh stains immediately with cold water alone, then with cold water mixed with glycerin. Rinse with vinegar if stain remains, then wash the garment with detergent in hot water.

Blood: Blood can be removed by presoaking garment in cold water for 45 minutes. Then wash in detergent and bleach which is safe for fabric, using cold water.

Fruit Juice: Sponge immediately with cold water, then presoak in cold water for 40 minutes. Wash garment in detergent with bleach which is safe for all fabrics.

Grass: Remove by presoaking garment in cold water for 40 minutes. Wash in hot water using detergent with a bleach which is safe for fabric. For colored fabrics, use two parts water to one part alcohol.

Lipstick: Remove by using a non-flammable dry cleaning solvent. Rub in detergent until stain is gone. Then wash garment in hot water.

Perspiration: Remove by taking old stains out with vinegar. Take new stains out with ammonia. First presoak in cold water, then rinse garment. Wash in hot water, using bleach if fabric is yellowed. For odor, sponge with colorless mouthwash.

To Remove Burned-on Starch from your iron, sprinkle salt on a sheet of waxed paper and move the iron back and forth several times. Then polish it with silver polish until the roughness or stain is removed.

Weights & Measures

3 teaspoons = 1 tablespoon

4 tablespoons = 1/4 cup

5-1/3 tablespoons = 1/3 cup

16 tablespoons = 1 cup

1 cup = 1/2 pint

4 cups = 1 quart

4 quarts = 1 gallon

1 ounce = 2 tablespoons or 1/8 cup

2 ounces = 4 tablespoons or 1/4 cup

8 ounces = 1 cup

16 ounces = 1 pound

32 ounces = 1 quart

Butter or Other Fat

1 ounce = 2 tablespoons

2 ounces = 1/4 cup or 4 tablespoons

1/4 pound = 1/2 cup

1/2 pound = 1 cup

1 pound = 2 cups

Lemons/Limes

1 medium = 2 to 3 tablespoons

5-8 medium = 1 cup

1 lemon rind = 1 tablespoon grated

Rice

1/3 cup uncooked = 1 cup cooked
2 cups uncooked = 6 cups cooked

Recipe Index